Pr

FA~~CE~~ ~~~~ .

MW00576366

"Simple beauty and authenticity is Holly's book of hope, transparency and faith. It's freshness will make you smile as you relate your own experiences with hers. Through trials – comes a life few understand. I pray you will be filled with that life "more abundantly" as you enjoy this work of God."

—Dr. Thelma Wells (aka Mama T), Former Speaker at Women of Faith Conferences, Author

"I've met people from all 197 countries in the world, but Holly Curby is one I will always remember! She is a fearless leader who inspires others to take action and has now taken her lessons in life to help all of us in this profound book. Don't hesitate. Buy this book now and it will be your new favorite companion for navigating life in a purposeful way."

—Garrett Gravesen, World-Renowned Speaker and International Best-Selling Author of "*10 Seconds of Insane Courage*"

"Be prepared to laugh and cry (sometimes on the same page) as you delve into Holly's deeply personal story of God's never-ending presence throughout all of life's unexpected twists and turns. The difficulties of life are shared without pretense in a raw and transparent way that anyone can connect with, dotted with humor and reality checks along the way. This is a message of hope in the midst of a series of daunting personal experiences that would send many into an unhealthy pattern of placing shame and blame on God and others so that we could then justifiably claim our spot in the victim's seat for the remainder of life. But Holly shares a different perspective with a heartfelt desire to use her experiences to encourage those who find themselves facing their own difficult days. This is ultimately a story of God's love and provision in whatever comes our way; it's also a story of examining and refining belief and faith when we're tested by fire. I encourage you to take this journey with Holly. You'll walk away being encouraged and hopeful that, no matter what comes your way, healing is possible and God is ever present, even on our darkest days."

—Tina Toombs Pelton, women's pastor and pastor of counseling and community ministries at Risen Life Church, Salt Lake City, Utah

"Holly lives exactly as she writes—with a passion for Jesus and sharing Him with others. Her positive take on difficult circumstances she's endured comes from a strong faith and trusting in God's word. Her writing is refreshing and offers encouragement for others who are down or discouraged. I highly recommend *Face-Lift* if you are in a season of difficulty—or just need a reminder of the peace that God can bring."

—Debbie Ward, Retired Director of Business Services for Utah-Idaho SBC and Salt Lake Baptist Association

"How can a series of such heartbreaking, would-be life shattering tragedies be turned into a great adventure with the Lord? Holly has learned practical ways to entrust her life, and the lives of her children, to God through her pain. And she has seen God use that pain to produce pearls—a string of glowing pearls—to hold near to her own heart and to share with others as a testimony of God's goodness and power."

—Judy McCoin, retired Bible study fellowship teacher of twenty-eight years

"Holly embodies a steadfast perseverance. As she walks you through so many heartbreaking seasons in her life, you will find hope is what pulled her through and can be found in everyday situations you might face. Her stories can help you grow, heal, and keep going amidst life's toughest struggles."

—LeighAnn Billsten, owner of Southern States Realty Group

"The 'fuller of cloth' and 'refiner of silver' is unfailingly present throughout Holly's purifying and transcendent journey told within these pages. Through her personal stories of unwavering reaching for God within her furnace of affliction, she brings hope and inspiration for us on our own bumpy footpaths towards Him. Through this book, we can come to know with faith and conviction, as Holly does, that 'God's got us.'"

—Susan Carlson, wife, mother, and garden-variety follower of Jesus Christ

"Have you ever thought, 'Things can't get any worse!' and then they do? What do you do? Where do you turn? Welcome to Holly's life. Dealing with life situations completely out of her control, she turned to the ultimate source of comfort, guidance, and assurance—God. She shares not only her story, but how she endured and grew stronger through God's Word and His enduring love. Hers is an ongoing witness to God's amazing love for us."

—Sherrie Walker, retired elementary school teacher

"I started reading *Face-Lift* as soon as I had access to a copy. The book did not disappoint. . . . I could not put it down. I felt as if I were right there with Holly, experiencing the feelings, fears, and frustrations that she was having. But what I loved the most was the fact that no matter what she was going through, she praised her Lord and Savior. Even when she didn't understand the 'why,' she kept a positive attitude and looked for the sun (Son). Holly has a gift of connecting with her readers. When she cried, I cried; when she laughed, I laughed!

"Holly lets the reader enter her world, showing that she genuinely cares and wants to minister to the needs of others. Holly gives room at the end of each chapter so the reader can think of their own lives and what they can learn from the lessons Holly shared. I can see this book being used worldwide for personal and group Bible studies. I highly recommend this book be added to your personal library. Better yet, give a copy to a friend! It is a must-have!!"

—Linda Padgett Schiele, Small-Business Owner of PostNet

"God is weaving a tapestry in all of our lives, only we can't yet see the beauty. In our day-to-day lives, we see threads out of place—threads of all different colors that look like chaos. But God, the designer of our lives and holder of our futures, knows when and where to place these seemingly random, scary, and miraculous moments.

"In *Face-Lift*, we can see the threads of Holly's life. Some threads are tragic, some are hopeful, but all are serving the purpose that God has intended for Holly's life. This encounter with the life of Holly and her family prompts change in all of us. It makes us answer questions we would perhaps not wish to pursue. It brings us around to being face-to-face with God and trusting in his timing and purpose. It reminds us of our need for community and our responsibility to be an encouragement to others.

"The hard-fought wisdom Holly has earned inspires us to live a more intentional life of serving the Lord and others through our own hardships and victories."

—Jessica Lane, Wife and Mother

Face-Lift:
Embracing Hope through your Heartaches
by Holly Curby

Published by

◤ köehlerbooks™

3705 Shore Drive
Virginia Beach, VA 23455
800-435-4811
www.koehlerbooks.com

Face-Lift

Embracing Hope
through your Heartaches

HOLLY CURBY

VIRGINIA BEACH
CAPE CHARLES

For my mother, who inspired this book.
My family, who is my core and who lived this alongside me.
My children, Allee and Peyton,
who are my heart's desire and my gift from God.
My prayer warriors, for their worn knees on my behalf.
To God, who is my foundation, who has always seen me
through . . . may YOU receive all glory, honor, and praise.
What's the most important thing about life?
Having Jesus in your heart.

CONTENTS

Note from The Author 4

Chapter 1: In the Beginning 7

Chapter 2: Change Is Hard 18

Chapter 3: Isolation Isn't Easy 30

Chapter 4: Heartache Is Painful 42

Chapter 5: Poison Leads to Forgiveness 54

Chapter 6: Cancer Is Devastating 70

Chapter 7: Waging War Is Exhausting 90

Chapter 8: Letting Go Brings Healing 104

Chapter 9: The Pandemic Was Challenging 126

Chapter 10: Blessings Are a Gift 140

Chapter 11: Living Life Anyway 162

Acknowledgements 165

Group Discussion Guide 170

How to Share Your Story (Testimony)..................177

How to Create a Personal Mission Statement...............181

Scripture Memory Verses....................185

Resource Recommendations......................197

Endnotes....................199

About the Author....................203

Let's Connect....................206

Huntsman Cancer Foundation.....................208

Notes....................209

Note from The Author

I MUST CONFESS, back in November of 2008, I had no clue how to use this new social media avenue called Facebook. In fact, my first post was literally, "Holly is enjoying watching her little one [daughter] run around and chase her brother"—and by brother, I was referring to our dog. So, fast-forward a decade, I was surprised at the many responses from my friends commenting about how they enjoyed my genuine posts, found encouragement in my vulnerability, related to various hurdles, and even suggested I write a book.

During that decade of navigating this new social media platform, I faced many challenges in life, which will be further unpacked as we connect throughout this book. It was through these trials, though, that I learned to use this outlet as an avenue to be real and raw, a safe haven for people to see that it's okay not to be okay. A reminder that we can feel tough emotions, walk through challenging times, have a difference in views and opinions but still show respect for each other. A place where we can be optimistic in the life lessons we can learn from our circumstances and a place where we can even encourage one another along life's journey.

Now please note, I am no philosopher or theologian. I'm simply a woman who loves the Lord and one who has lived a lot of life in a short amount of time. Life happens to all of us, though—that's no surprise. Through any trial that comes, I have consistently tried to embrace the perspective, if I have to go through this, then I want to:

1. Glorify God in and through it

2. Learn and grow from it

After all, if God brings us to it, He can bring us through it, right? And His plan for our life can far exceed the circumstances we find ourselves in today.

My hope and prayer as you read *Face-Lift* is that it will have parts that encourage you, others that will inspire you, and some that will provide resources to help equip you in whatever season of life you are in.

Each chapter includes my personal story, an action step to help provide self-reflection and application from that chapter, a Facebook post from that particular season of life (except the first two chapters where it didn't exist yet), and then concludes with a face-lift "moral of the story" Bible verse that I encourage you to memorize. These memory verses are also found as tear-outs in the back of the book so that after each chapter you can take that verse and physically place it somewhere that will help you memorize it throughout your day or week. If you'd like to go deeper, or if you are reading *Face-Lift* with a group, then be sure to check out the Personal Guide/Discussion Guide located toward the end of the book.

I realize you could be reading a thousand other books, so please hear me say thank you. Thank you for choosing *Face-Lift*. Thank you for allowing me to come alongside you. Thank you for investing time in this journey together.

During this time, I would welcome you to picture us strolling along a path in a beautiful park or garden together. Throughout each chapter, we'll discover something new as we walk along the path, but then we can stop and rest on a nearby bench and let what we've just shared soak in, taking as much time as we need. You'll find that, throughout this stroll, we will chat about how to be real in a social media world, reminding each other that we are not alone and we can survive the circumstances of life—and even thrive in them. Most importantly, we will come to embrace peace and comfort knowing that we can have hope in the One who can be the lifter of our head, resulting in no matter what comes our way, having a total face-lift.

Now, let's go enjoy the journey.

Chapter 1

In the Beginning

IT WAS 2009 when a representative from the national Women of Faith conferences flew out to Utah to meet with me. I had been promoting Women of Faith conferences for years and had a decent response in attendees each year. As a result, this woman was coming out to thank me, encourage me, pray with me, and probably ensure the promotion of future conferences would continue. I recall very vividly sitting beside her on the brown leather couch in the foyer of my church and saying, "I feel God is calling me to Women's Ministry. I just don't know what that looks like." At the time, I didn't understand how God could use me in such a ministry; after all, I came from what I would say was the perfect upbringing in a solid Christian home with two faithful God-loving parents. I felt I was raised in a Pollyanna world, so how could I encourage and empathize with others who had experiences I couldn't relate to? Little did I know that God was preparing my heart for the journey ahead, which would equip me for such a ministry.

It was that very next year that God would start leading me through deep preparation. He would take me from my comfort zone and stretch me in ways that felt painful, harmful, and dangerous so that He could refine me, mold me, and make me into who He needed me to be. He was preparing me and encouraging me to reach out to others with relatability and empathy.

When the weight of life's challenges seemed to be too much—experiencing personal health issues, relationship strains, applying for government assistance of insurance, unemployment, and food, family illnesses, spiritual battles, and even death—God would once again reach down and graciously lift my face. Through it all, I was reminded that where God calls you, He'll equip you.

We all have a story to tell, scars from various battles of life that we could compare to each other's, but that's not the purpose of this book nor the purpose of our wounds. As we navigate our way through this thing called life, we have choices to make. Do we run from the challenges we face, going through them kicking and screaming, or do we seek to learn and grow as we are refined in the fire? For me, I chose the latter, and my social media became my reminder to keep pressing on and living even during my darkest days. I often even had to remind myself that what was feeling like my personal journal was publicly displayed on Facebook. What I didn't expect from this avenue was for my posts to have reviews of how my life experiences were actually encouraging others. Through such humbling comments, I found my purpose in the midst of my storms, to shine a light of hope to others through my vulnerability and rawness of life.

Perhaps this book can relate and empathize with the road you are on, provide a comfort that you are not alone on your journey, and encourage you to press through whatever lies ahead. Just as a king acknowledged those before him by the lifting of one's head, so may our King reach down and meet you where you are and give you a face-lift.

I figure we might as well get acquainted a little bit, seeing as you're reading this book. My name is Holly. I was raised by a preacher and a school teacher. My father was senior pastor of the churches we served until I was thirty years old and, even then, continued to serve as counsel for churches after retirement. My mother, an elementary school teacher for twenty-five years, served faithfully alongside him. My sister Christy, the oldest child, brother Scott, the middle child, and I, the baby, were always taught that we were saved to serve, not just to sit; so, we did.

Our weeks consisted of much time together, most often at church or gathered around the dinner table at home. Speaking of which, meals were always interesting in our home. It was the norm for me to bring a friend home from church on a Sunday to join us for lunch, and as we gathered around the table prepared to feast, my dad would look at my friend with a mischievous grin on his face, and depending on what the main entrée was for that meal, he'd say something like, "Have you ever eaten frog eyes?" Did I mention the frequency of each friend joining us for a meal seemed, coincidently enough, to average one visit per person? As if you couldn't tell, dad's favorite holiday is April Fool's Day, as his coworkers could attest, and he never seemed to disappoint. One of my nephews was even born on April Fool's Day (that brought dad much joy, as you can imagine), and he, too, has inherited the April Fool's gene, but I digress.

As I mentioned, we were raised in church. I was seven years old when I came to know Christ as my personal Lord and Savior. It was my father who led me to Christ. It is my father who has always been the leader of my home, the shepherd of our church, my wise counsel, and my solid rock. I was raised feeling loved, safe, that I belonged, and possessing a sense that God had a special path for me.

Throughout life's path, I've always wanted to push myself, to see what was beyond the boundaries or limitations as I saw them—not out of disobedience or competition but out of a desire to know what I'm capable of doing. This is probably where the achiever in me shows up (visit gallup.com to take your personality assessment). I was in seventh grade when I entered a short story competition in our local district public school. I performed *The Monkey's Paw* as a monologue, and to my amazement, not only did I win the competition, but I realized I loved performing. I went on to play lead roles in my high school theatre productions, take professional acting classes, write plays and skits for our church, direct dinner theaters for the community, and even work as an extra in a few movies. I found that as I stepped into the shoes of scripted parts, I felt full of life and confidence—a passion and fulfillment of my purpose.

As much as I loved to shine on stage, I have had my fair share of public embarrassments and insecurities. I was seven years old when I was baptized. Back in the day when handrails were optional, I stepped into the church baptistry filled with water, my father awaiting my arrival at the bottom step, and I slipped on a step, falling down the stairs, with a huge splash at the end. As my dad kept asking if I was okay, I remember turning to see a church full of people with all eyes on me. Yep, embarrassment officially entered my emotional experiences.

Along with embarrassment, I have definitely faced challenges of insecurities—from feeling overweight and very aware of my gummy smile to being self-conscious of my singing after a rejection my first time trying out for the ensemble team in high school. I am flawed, just like everybody else. Those insecurities still follow me even now, as an adult. Isn't it interesting how such rejections and experiences in life can stick with us for years to come?

Despite my flaws, I come from a family who believes Christ will strengthen us through all things. This mindset popped up often during childhood—when I was in bed traction from a childhood hip disease at the same time my brother underwent emergency kidney surgery, when the family vacation was interrupted by my dad's mom in her final days, her passing away just weeks before my sister's wedding, watching the heartache when my sister was left at the alter (her groom's sudden fear of marriage presenting on the day of the wedding), and when my mom's doctors feared she had cervical cancer.

Yes, my family is no stranger to life's difficulties, and yet these and many other challenges not listed were faced as a family and with our faith. The grounded family upbringing of my Christian parents, who were God-fearing people and faithful to each other and the Lord, had prepared us for any battle fought. The heroes of my life have always been my family—my dad, my mom, my sister, and my brother—and, of course, my knight in shining armor being the Lord Himself.

As with most things, one doesn't always realize what they have until it's gone. During eighth grade, I felt laid upon my heart to adopt as my life verse:

"Trust in the Lord with all your heart and lean not on your own understanding; in all your ways submit to him, and he will make your path straight."

PROVERBS 3:5-6

Little did I know that regardless of my faith being my foundation and my family being my core, I would embark upon much in my life that would require me to relinquish all understanding of what was happening, and I'd have to fully trust God with and in all challenges. Warren Wiersbe said, "A faith that cannot be tested cannot be trusted,"[1] and as my dad once shared in one of his messages, "You won't ever come to the beginning of God until you come to the end of yourself." Yes, I would be tested, and I would come to the end of myself, where I'd find myself prostrate before the throne of God, who would mercifully and graciously be the lifter of my head. Dear ones, this same Lord can lift your face as well—and such is my purpose and prayer in sharing my story with you.

Now it's your turn. Pretend you and I just grabbed a coffee or tea from the vendor in the park. We reach the first bench and take a seat. Would you mind sharing a bit about yourself? What has influenced your life in being who you are today? What are some memories that stand out in your mind? This is where I encourage you to do a little self-discovery. What is your story? Where does your story begin, and how did you get to where you are now? God tells us in Jeremiah 29:11 that He knows the plans He has for us. He does not want us to suffer, rather He wants to show us hope and provide for us a future. God can use every bit of who you are— from your pain and embarrassments to your joys and triumphs— since, after all, He is the ultimate author of your story. When we discover who we are and vulnerably bring to light our fears and failures, our passions and pains, our triumphs and tributes, it is then that we can humble ourselves and use our past not to define us but rather to see the hope that God has given and help us create that future. After all, "God can't lift an unbowed head."[2]

Face-Lift Action Step #1

MAKE A TIMELINE of your life below. From birth until this day, mark your major high points in life as well as your major low points. For each point, write the names of those who were instrumental in that moment. As you reflect on this timeline, what did you learn during each high and low point? Remember, none of what you've been through is a surprise to God, and He can intentionally use it for good while preparing you for your purpose in the future.

HIGHS

BIRTH   NOW

LOWS

Who were instrumental people?

_____
_____
_____
_____
_____

What were some formative moments?

_____
_____
_____
_____
_____

What have you learned from your experiences?

_____
_____
_____
_____
_____

How has your timeline impacted who you are and where you are today?

_____
_____
_____
_____
_____

As you reflect on your completed timeline, what do you notice? Did anything surprise you?

_____

_____

_____

_____

_____

Are there any reoccurring themes? Blessings in disguise? Situations that still stick with you? What do you learn about yourself?

_____

_____

_____

_____

If you have a motto or life quote, share it below. What inspired it?

_____

_____

_____

_____

Face-Lift #1

In the beginning,
God has good for us

"'For I know the plans I have for you,'
declares the Lord,
'plans to prosper you and not to harm you,
plans to give you hope and a future.'"

—JEREMIAH 29:11

Chapter 2

Change Is Hard

I WAS IN eighth grade when I met him. We clashed at first, but soon this boy would become my best friend. Our friendship grew, and before we knew it, we had been dating eight years. My parents had always advised me, "Marry your best friend, and make sure you've seen each other in many aspects of life prior to marriage." All of which we had experienced. From ailments, illnesses, and loved ones' deaths to graduations, job losses, and overall rough patches, I felt we had seen each other through many angles. Although we both knew marriage was on the table, we had never discussed it; we just knew we wanted to pursue our collegiate degrees, serve together in our church, and get settled into a career prior to getting married.

One day while working in the mall management office at a local regional shopping center, one of our fine jewelry tenants ran up to me, grabbed my hand, and asked to see "it." She could obviously tell by the confused look on my face, and the bare finger she was inspecting, that a proposal had not yet taken place. Although the jeweler ruined the surprise of getting engaged, the actual proposal moment, marking the beginning of such a major change in my life, was far from ruined.

That very weekend, as my boyfriend and I drove to have dinner on a yacht, I knew this must be the night. I remember being so nervous and wanting time to stand still. As we boarded the vessel, I was in awe—the interior décor was elegant, the four-course meal was delicious, and the stars were brightly shining with just the softest breeze blowing across our faces. It was perfect. Suddenly, he knelt to one knee and proposed. I don't even recall a word he said, but I do remember hearing the instrumental to the song "How Great Thou Art" playing overhead, and I took it as a sign from God that this was the next step on my journey.

Almost a year later, there I was, a bride preparing to walk down the aisle to be wed. I recall ever so vividly looking at my reflection in the mirror, smiling, and saying, "Let's do this," and then I took the arm of my father, who would walk me down a flowered path to stand before our family and friends in front of a majestic waterfall, the place my high school sweetheart and I would say, "I do." An evening celebration with food and dancing followed—a magical and perfect night. As we parted to the limo, my mother embraced me and whispered in my ear, "I hope you felt like a princess." I had the wedding of my dreams. Cinderella had nothing on me.

Years went by, and together we served in many areas of our church, leading youth group, as deacon/deaconess, and even hosting Bible study groups in our home. We both were settled in our careers and so happily in love. A couple of years passed, and we got that exciting news that we were adding to our family—I was going to be a momma. Other than some food allergies developing, pregnancy was going smooth, and life just felt perfect.

The night before my baby shower, I was trying to finish up some last-minute work on our home computer when I accidentally accessed the wrong account and came across some startling emails. As I opened each one, I felt sick to my stomach. Suddenly, my Pollyanna world shattered. Perhaps you can relate? Life seemed to be going along seamlessly, and then it wasn't.

Looking back, I should have reached out for help at our church—the pastor (who, remind you, was also my dad), or a fellow deacon, anyone. Instead, I did the worst thing someone in such a situation could do. Following an in-depth and emotional conversation with my husband, I never spoke a word to anyone about what I had found. I buried it deep within me as if it was a hidden secret I hoped no one would ever find. Unbeknownst to me, Satan entered our marriage in a mighty way that night. I no longer looked at my husband the same way. I lost a trust in him that damaged our marriage. I allowed bitterness and resentment to creep in. As much as I thought it was just a bad dream, reality was the storm brewing, and it was only getting worse.

Oh, precious one, please learn from my failure. We are shown an example of how to deal with sin in Matthew 18:15-17.

1. Confront the person (verse 15).

2. If they do not listen, then take someone with you to confront them (verse 16).

3. If they still refuse to change of their ways, then bring it before the church (verse 17a).

4. Lastly, if they won't even listen to the church, then step away (verse 17b).

Keep in mind that, in each account, we are to approach others gently and meekly, with the goal of restoration (Galatians

6:1). Even if the confrontation goes well, you may still need professional help from a counselor or therapist. My silence did not win over my husband; it simply covered the sin and allowed for Satan to have a foothold, becoming a giant in my life.

What giant are you facing in your life? Our giants can have different faces: fear, anxiety, anger, control, rejection, people-pleasing, avoiding conflict—the list goes on and on. Do you recall the biblical story of David? The youngest shepherd of eight brothers, who was simply obeying his father by taking food to his brothers in battle, was the only one brave enough to step up to Goliath, the giant. And with only a slingshot and some pebbles in his hand, he defeated that giant!

All too often, instead of facing our giant, we have a tendency to hide from them, run away from them, give in to them, or even pretend they don't exist. Well, do you know what happens then? Our giants will rob us of our joy, zap our strength, hold us captive in our bondage to them, and prevent us from reaching our full potential. They can even keep us from following the path God has for us. Most of all, as my parents used to always caution us kids, "If you don't face your giants, they are only going to get bigger!" Oh, friend, won't we remember in times of challenges and trials, when our giants rear their ugly head, "It's not the height of our giant but the size of our God"[3] that matters. Don't let Satan have a foothold in your life. Speak up, reach out, and seek help.

A couple of months later, my giant faded into the shadows of other challenges to be faced. It was time for my daughter's debut, and in the midst of her coming, I passed out once during labor and once following labor. Shortly after delivering her, I began to go into shock from the loss of blood and was unable to hold her until they could find the source of the blood loss in my body. Then a nurse came in and told us our daughter may have Down syndrome. Come to find out, the hospital had missed a diagnosis the prior week; therefore, the nurses were just on high alert. It was quite a whirlwind experience, but days later, as we left the hospital, I felt our little growing family have a fresh start. Despite the damage discovered during my pregnancy, I still believed I had a wonderful marriage with my husband and felt so blessed in life. Each night as we'd lay down to sleep, I'd turn toward my husband and, with deep gratitude, tell him, "We are so blessed." I loved our life together—serving in the church, living down the street from my parents, raising our precious daughter, and both having solid jobs that provided great support and stability. Although we had a hiccup in the road, we were, as I envisioned, a picture-perfect family.

About this time, social media became popular. I eased into it, completely misunderstanding how to do a post on Facebook. I even attempted to start a blog, but I really knew nothing of its purpose or the time commitment it would take to keep up with it. What I didn't plan on is how this new social media outlet would come to impact my life in the years and trials to come. This one avenue would soon play such a major role in my life, serving as a direct influence for this very book and acting as a catalyst for my role in a ministry I couldn't have fathomed to take part in otherwise.

A few years and many Facebook posts later, we learned that our family was growing once again. We were unexpectedly expecting our second child. As excited as we were, fears resurfaced from what I had discovered the night before my daughter's baby shower. I was insecure and fearful that history would repeat itself. I became paranoid, questioning my husband's late home arrivals and long work weekends and constantly looking at his phone. I shared my concerns with him, feeling guilty for my feelings and developing an unhealthy codependency within the marriage.

As much as I wanted to reach out for help, too much was going on to even stay afloat. My dad had survived a heart attack two years prior to my son's birth, and shortly after that, he announced his full-time pastoral retirement in the fall of 2010. We were excited for my dad, as we knew he deserved and needed some refresher time, not from serving God (we know he'll continue to do that all the days of his life) but from the heavy demands of being a full-time pastor. Little did we realize, though, all the changes that would ripple down within our family at the same time—my mom was nearing retirement, my brother was up for a promotion as vice president of his company, my sister (who served as my dad's secretary for nine years) had mentioned that she was ready for something new, and I was expecting our second child. So, within a matter of two months, these worlds collided. My mom retired, my brother was promoted, my sister started a new job at her sons' elementary school, my dad retired, and I gave birth to our son.

The day I went into labor, as I lay in the hospital bed with the contractions coming quicker and quicker, my husband would often leave the room to take a call or send a text. He explained to me and those in the room that he needed to handle some work things, but just one glance at my sister's eyes made me feel like she knew that buried secret from years ago, and the fears that haunted me during this pregnancy.

I'm not sure if it was my fears, my post-birth hormones, or just the major changes we were experiencing, but during so many celebrations, I felt a deep loss from my life. We—a family who had served in church together for my thirty years of life—were now not only faced with our father not being the leader of our church flock anymore but also the reality that, out of respect for the next pastor and his family, our family needed to find a new church home. Allowing the incoming pastor to step in as the new shepherd or leader of the church is often an act of pastoral etiquette. We had experienced some pivotal life moments in this church, and these church members were our friends, our church family—experiencing graduations, weddings, births—and now we had to find a new church home. The anxiety set upon us (at least it did in the women of the family), and we tried to savor the final memories of our time together in that church. Perhaps you can relate. Deep losses. Too much change, too quickly or all at once. Feeling pushed out of comfort zones and forced into the unknown. Or simply a loss of what *was* as you enter a season of what *is*.

Through all the emotions, I found comfort in:

2 a time to be born and a time to die,
   a time to plant and a time to uproot
4 a time to weep and a time to laugh,
   a time to mourn and a time to dance,
11 He has made everything beautiful in its time. He
   has also set eternity in the human heart; yet no one
   can fathom what God has done from beginning to
   end.

ECCLESIASTES 3:2, 4, 11.

And in:

Even to your old age and gray hairs I am he,
I am he who will sustain you.
I have made you and I will carry you;
I will sustain you and I will rescue you.

ISAIAH 46:4.

I was reminded in Ecclesiastes 3:1 that the timing of everything occurring was perfectly designed. My heart's desire was to not go into labor until after dad retired so that I could take in each of my last Sundays at church. My sister and I were also heavily involved in an appreciation banquet for that church, which took place the day after dad's last day behind the pulpit, and we wanted to see that through to completion. Since our family tends to travel as a herd, it was also important to me that my family would be able to be at the hospital for my son's birth, as we'd done for all the grandkids, and my brother had a huge holiday weekend sale coming up at his work that he couldn't miss. Gratefully, God knew all of these desires in my heart, and as result of His timing, we were all able to attend Dad's last Sunday, I was able to complete my partnership with my sister at the banquet before I went into labor (at the banquet, might I add), and I delivered our sweet precious boy with my entire family at the hospital. That, my friend, is nothing we could have planned. That's God's timing. God knows the desires of your heart, too.

If I could encourage you through all the changes you may be facing, it would be this—trust in God's timings, then watch for God to show up, and count every blessing you see. We may not be able to understand His ways, but we can always trust His heart.

Face-Lift Action Step #2

WHAT CHANGES OR challenges have you overcome in life? What promises of God did you see during that time? What changes or challenges are you facing right now? What blessings are you seeing from God during these hardships? So often, we overlook the lightness amid times of darkness. So go ahead and remind yourself of His goodness and power - let His light shine.

Changes /Challenges Overcome	Promises Seen

Changes /Challenges Currently in Life	Blessings

Reflect on your list of current changes and challenges. Are any of them a Goliath in your life—a giant you need to defeat today? Put an exclamation mark next to those giants. Now, proclaiming as David did, replace the first underlined parts of David's prayer with your changes/challenges you've overcome and the giant you marked in the last underlined portion.

"The Lord who rescued me from the paw of the lion and the paw of the bear [your changes/ challenges overcome] will rescue me from the hand of this Philistine [your giant from current changes/ challenges]"

1 SAMUEL 17:37A.

Just as David proclaimed to the Philistines—go fight your giants in the name of the Lord Almighty.

Face-Lift #2

Change Is Hard—
Trust Him

"Trust in the Lord with all your heart and lean
not on your own understanding;
in all your ways submit to him, and he will
make your paths straight."

—PROVERBS 3:5-6

Chapter 3

Isolation Isn't Easy

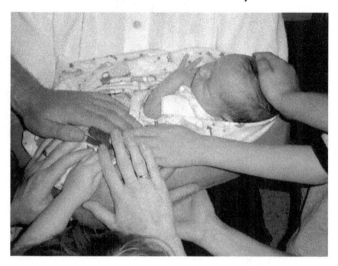

THE SUNDAY AFTER my son was born was my dad's birthday and also the first Sunday we officially had no church home. So, our family decided to meet for a time of worship at my parents' house. My dad had asked us to each be prepared to read a verse that God had laid on our hearts, and Mom would provide lunch.

Although my husband and I only lived four houses down from my parents, my brother called to comically inform us that seats were filling up fast, and parking spaces were limited. Our previous church had a sweet man who would always provide donuts, fruit, juices, and coffee on Sunday mornings. So, attempting to add a little norm to the morning, Mom followed suit with her own spread of cinnamon rolls and coffee, and we added fruit and donuts.

As we began the service, the view of this church was quite different than usual. Here we were walking to church, meeting in a home, and sitting in a combination of chairs, sofas, and piano benches, all arranged in a circle in my parents' living room. We were gathered around the piano and wearing all sorts of attire, my sister in camo pants, my dad in a bowtie. We proceeded with the service of scripture sharing, songs, my dad giving a sermon, and concluded with my son's baby dedication – a commitment by me and my husband to raise him according to God's word. I kept finding myself in awe of the morning. We didn't meet in the typical church building, and there wasn't an attendance record kept, but we worshiped as a family and sang praises to our Heavenly Father. It was truly a morning unlike any other. I kept thanking God for my family, and most of all for my parents raising us in the center of God's will. That morning, my eyes were opened even more. It isn't about where you go to church or where you hold church but about being a part of the family of God. I will forever cherish our one day of church at my parents' home with the congregation consisting of just our family.

Does this sound familiar? Perhaps life circumstances have kept you from walking in to the actual four walls of a church building. That's okay. You can still worship without being in the presence of a brick-and-mortar building. As defined in Webster's dictionary, worship is simply the "act of paying divine honors to the Supreme Being."[4] It goes on to say that this act of worship involves adoration, acts of reverence, and is often accompanied by prayer. Friend, you can worship as you sing in the shower, as you take a walk in the park, or even as you sit in traffic on the interstate. The important thing to remember is that we do not give up meeting together as referenced in Hebrews 10:25. These days, we have so many resources available to us. We can meet together in a home or coffee shop, we can attend church online and stream sermons, and we can even gather in small groups at church members' homes. The purpose is to continue to meet together.

My mother shared a story with me as to why it's so important to still meet within the church. She shared that the zebra's predator can easily identify the zebra and therefore attack them when they are separated from their herd. However, when a herd of zebra are all together, the predator simply cannot make them out to attack—their stripes confuse the predator. Friend, we are that zebra. When we are joined in the fellowship of the church body, we are no longer easy prey. If we aren't careful, we can find ourselves in our own self-made isolation. It is often in solitude where we feed on our fears instead of our faith.

Little did I know, my fears were about to be tested during this season. A couple of months had passed since that special Sunday morning service in my parents' home, and Thanksgiving was upon us. It was the first holiday for my son and, yes, another reason to gather the whole herd for a family get-together. Shortly after the festivities, I began to feel unwell. At first, it was just keeping me in the restroom, but then I noticed hives developing all over my body. We went to the hospital, and they couldn't quite figure out what triggered the reactions, but they confirmed I was having an allergic reaction. After treating me, they sent me home. In the days that followed, anytime and anything I ate would break me out in hives. We soon found ourselves at an allergy specialist who, after conducting many tests over a couple of weeks, diagnosed me with some food allergies and idiopathic anaphylaxis (basically, an unknown reason why my body goes into anaphylaxis reactions, but it does). The plan was to restart my body's eating pattern. I was to start with rice for every meal and introduce a new ingredient every three days. After three days of rice-only meals, come day four, I added salt to my rice (and ate it for all meals for three more days). Day seven, I added peas to my rice and salt (for another three days). And that system continued. I left the doctor's office in tears and utterly discouraged. I followed that prescription to a tee though, and in addition to losing double digits in weight, I did find myself free of reactions, so I came to the realization that this was my new normal. Meals panicked me. Would what I ate settle? Would I be near a medical facility should I have a reaction? I began to live in fear of food and leaving my home.

Throughout the next year, I kept a daily food journal, tracking what I ate, any symptoms experienced, and a list of go-to foods and meals for when I felt overwhelmed or panicked when meal planning. I hit a point of despair, unsure I was going to live through this trial. I had gone through health challenges before. In addition to my Legg-Calve-Perthes hip disease as a child, I needed to have my gallbladder removed shortly after having my first child, but this allergy health challenge seemed never-ending. It felt isolating from what I once enjoyed doing—eating out. It felt scary as I feared the unknown consequences of eating. It felt imprisoning as I was fearful of being out alone and having a reaction. That's when I decided to turn to what prompted this book—social media, specifically my Facebook page.

Now, please don't hear me wrong. Through all my life, I've always turned to God for His peace, direction, comfort, and healing. In addition, I have always been involved in Bible studies and daily devotional time with the Lord, but social media was a different outlet for me. I decided I would no longer post about what I was doing, but I would instead use it to reach out to those I felt I had wronged—those I needed to seek forgiveness from—but also to encourage anyone reading my Facebook timeline to do the same and to be intentional.

What are you going through in life where God may be using the time to get your attention to take action, reach out, or perhaps simply find rest and "be still" (Psalm 46:10)?

Throughout that year, I began to feel an overwhelming peace from God. Just as the poem, "Thanksgiving Observance," by an unknown author goes:

"Count your blessings instead of your crosses.
Count your gains instead of your losses.
Count your joys instead of your woes.
Count your friends instead of your foes.
Count your smiles instead of your tears.
Count your courage instead of your fears.
Count your full years instead of your lean.
Count your kind deeds instead of your mean.
Count your health instead of your wealth.
Count on God instead of yourself."[5]

I was seeing that play out in my life. He provided reconciliation with some friendships, healing from others, and I felt the ending of that poem along with 1 Corinthians 1:26-27 coming to fruition—that through relying on God's strength and not my own, He was using my weakness for His glory. I was getting the hang of this eating thing. I was enjoying being a mother of two little ones, and I was loving being a wife who eagerly tried to serve her husband.

I had felt a heaviness on my heart to pray for my husband in a new way, for the Lord to use whatever means possible to grow him into a man after God's own heart, as well as for my own spiritual growth. I was heavily involved in a weekly women's Bible study group at church. I found serenity in my time with the Lord each day. I once again felt like life was perfect. I don't believe in precognition, yet I have always had a feeling of "sixth sense," where I probably read too much into things. Okay, I definitely read too much into things. Have you ever seen those signs that read, "Wait while I overthink this?" Yep—that's me. Although this wisdom or insight (as some might call it) is often right and therefore has helped me in some decision-making, it also scares me when I feel that the "other shoe" is about to drop.

As the seasons were changing, and in attempt to overcome

these months of hibernation, I had decided to take the kids and the dog out for some good physical exercise with a walk in the park. After a pleasant afternoon, we headed back to the car, when I noticed our 135-pound Goldendoodle, Dakoda, was limping. I took him to the vet for a quick checkup, and the doctor assured us it was just a sprain from too much walking that day. After days of Dakoda continuing to limp, the doctor requested that we bring him back in for what was at worst a fracture somewhere in the leg. My husband took him back to the vet, and I took the kids to go support my nephew at his baseball game. As I drove to the game, that sixth sense kicked in, and I called my husband, fearing the worst. Sure enough, I heard those words from my husband across the cell phone connection—"The doctor thinks he has bone cancer." As I left the game later that day, rain came pouring down, and as the kids and I got loaded in the car, a song played on the radio, "Blessings" by Laura Story.[6] The lyrics still echo in my ears today regarding our trials in life perhaps being disguised as our blessings and mercies in life. Tears rolled down my face as I knew we were facing a challenging road, yet God's very presence was felt upon me as I knew He was in control. That next morning, I received a call from the vet confirming that the radiologist was sure it was bone cancer in Dakoda. You may be thinking, "It's a dog!" To me and my husband, he was our first child. Upon hearing this news, our hearts broke, and tears seemed to overflow my face once again.

Our vet had referred us to a specialized clinic, so off we went to meet with the cancer specialist for animals. Although we were told our dog would pass from the cancer, our goal was to help him be pain free. From that point on, we had many decisions to make. One vehicle needed replacing. My husband was working a lot of overtime to help pay the added bills. Our daughter was preparing to start preschool. And we were still seeking a church home since my dad's retirement. My dad has always said, "God is not the author of confusion but of clarity." So we tried to focus on facts, maintaining a goal to stick to what was best for Dakoda, and we turned it over to God, seeking His complete clarity in our future decisions.

The months that followed included chemotherapy and even a trip to Colorado for a specialist to amputate Dakoda's leg. Nothing seemed to be working, and then one November day, we got the call from the cancer specialist. Dakoda's cancer had spread, and Dakoda was most likely experiencing more pain than he let on. With that one call, we knew it was time to say goodbye to our beloved "first born." That Goldendoodle had been our one-year anniversary gift to each other. He had welcomed the birth of each of our human babies, helped protect them, and played with them as he allowed doggie back rides and pulled ears. He had brought such a sense of joy to our family. Over-personalizing things as I do, I saw the death of our anniversary gift as an indication of the changes about to take place in our marriage. That sixth sense ran over me like a horrible nightmare I couldn't wake up from. As much as I wanted to rest in the security of the life we had built together, I felt as if that other "shoe" was about to drop.

Perhaps you can relate. You continue to have one thing happen after another, and life just feels overwhelming. You have many decisions to make, and it all seems like too much. Just as you persevere one hurdle, another one comes, and you just aren't sure how much you have left in you. You feel alone. Deflated. Defeated. The enemy tries to discourage us, to isolate us.

But here's the thing. Don't. Give. Up!

When you feel yourself caving in and wanting to hide or escape the world, reach out. You don't have to do this thing called life alone. This is when we need our (zebra) herd the most.

Face-Lift Action Step #3

WHETHER AN INTROVERT or extrovert, we need people. We need a support team with whom we can share our struggles and celebrate our joys. Likewise, we need to be in someone else's corner too. No matter the season of life, there is always something we can do for others. We can spare time for a phone call, invite someone over to share a meal, or even send a card to say we care. Who can you call when you're feeling all alone, overwhelmed, or in need of advice or just a listening ear? Who can you show up for, love, and support? Now commit to call your team (herd)—and commit to show up for others. Remember, it's harder for the predator to attack when we huddle together.

My Support Team

1.

2.

3.

Those I Can Encourage

1.

2.

3.

Holly Harding Curby
December 6, 2011

Ever look back at your year and think, "Wow God! You are amazing!"? Well, that about sums up our year. Sometimes after we see the whole picture is when we realize why God doesn't reveal it to us all at once. Thank you God...we are so blessed.

Face-Lift #3

Isolation Isn't Easy—
You Are Not Alone

"Not giving up meeting together, as some
are in the habit of doing,
but encouraging one another—and all the
more as you see the Day approaching."

—HEBREWS 10:25

Chapter 4

Heartache Is Painful

HAVE YOU EVER had something so traumatizing take place that just the thought of it was painful? This is that chapter. It was the last chapter to complete, as I heavily avoided it, knowing vulnerability, a feeling of reliving painful memories, and hard decisions about what details to include would come along with it. And of course, I still want to do right by my former husband.

As I shared from the last chapter, my husband and I had been through a year of church searching as result of my dad retiring. We came upon a weekend where we had finally decided which church to join. It had been a beautiful weekend. My husband had been remodeling our upstairs bathroom, and it was finally complete. We spent the whole day in our jammies, watching movies with the kids while snuggling on the couch, and in the evening, we enjoyed turning on some music in the kitchen and dancing together. Reflecting on this weekend enhances my understanding of *enjoy the moment*—we aren't guaranteed tomorrow.

Little did I realize that my world, as I knew it, was about to shatter. The next morning, I awoke to hearing five words clearly. Five words that would forever change my life. Five words, crystal clear in my mind, loud and authoritative, stern yet said with care. Just as a shepherd would lead his sheep to protect them, I heard the direction of the Lord speak to me, saying, "Go look at his phone."

That directive would soon lead me to a whole new path of discovery. Painful conversations. Wise counsel sought. Countless tears shed. An unknown road to walk. A Sunday school teacher once asked us, "What will it take for you to stop serving God?" The teacher then stated, "Whatever it is, Satan will use to stop us." This was so profound to me, I even wrote it in my Bible. Then and there, I declared, "My family." Well, here I was, Satan on the attack for the very thing I held most dear. My initial response was that I wanted to save my marriage. I wanted my family back. I had no idea about the journey I was about to embark upon. I was terrified.

Social media no longer held a place in my life. I wanted to hide. I wanted to protect my husband from embarrassment and shame. I wanted to protect exposure from what had happened to my family. I wanted to spare myself criticism of people thinking I wasn't enough. I wanted to wake up from this nightmare.

After my discovery and a confronting conversation with my husband, we immediately found help through a counselor, who advised that my husband find an alternative place to stay for the weekend, prior to us meeting all together. Looking back, I believe that was the worst mistake we could have made. After my husband left that day, he never returned home, pushing us a step further from reconciliation.

I still remember trying to catch each breath. Life seemed so incomprehensible. The only way I was able to fall asleep was to literally hold my iPod speaker in my hands while encouraging hymns and praise songs played. Perhaps you've felt that way? That it is all you can do to stay afloat, to take that next breath, to survive the day.

Growing up, whenever we'd get sick, my mom would always remind us that nights were the hardest. Well, when we go through tough times and trials in life, that truth can still apply. Nights mean loneliness, darkness, and an inability to see clearly ahead of you. Oh, how we long for the light to shine, to brighten our path, to see life around us, and to not feel alone. As I prepared to walk this dark, lonely path ahead, my sister wisely instilled within me the reminder of an all-too familiar hymn that I'd encourage you to listen to. "Because HE lives, we CAN face tomorrow."[7]

Just as you may have asked during your darkest hour, I too cried out to God, "WHY?" As my husband proceeded to move out of the house, I couldn't help but fixate on his luggage—the very luggage we had used on a cruise together with our family just that prior year. The very luggage that once represented adventure and getting away together now represented separation and darkness. My heart hurt for my husband, and it hurt for us. I didn't want him to be alone, to be without, or to feel unloved. I packed his favorite foods, wrote a note of hope and support that we could get through this together, and then prayed over his things before he departed.

I will confess, though, the hardest thing I've ever done is to pray for another. I believe that prayer is both powerful and effective (James 5:16). I begged God to take what Satan had meant for harm, and to use it for His glory (Genesis 50:20). Along this path, I felt discouraged, trying to understand so many pieces to this puzzle. I'm so grateful God gives us only one piece of the puzzle at a time. If we knew the bigger picture, it may be too much. His timing is always best.

Before long, God laid on my heart three names. Three names I was to call upon, reach out to, and seek their support alongside this trial—to help hold me up just as Aaron and Hur did with Moses during his battle (Exodus 17:12). The next step, contacting them and letting them see the deepest wounds in my life, was one that took a massive step of obedience. One of the three people was a woman a few years older than me, someone I was in youth group with as a teenager. Another was a women's ministry leader at a local church whom I had only met once during our church searching after dad's retirement. The other was . . . the wife of my husband's high school best friend. I was terrified. Not only would the appearance of my perfect family be shattered, but I feared bringing such exposure upon my family.

Isn't it interesting how, when we fear that next step, God can often make it for us? I've learned I'd much rather bow to my knees in obedience than have them bowed for me. Shortly after God laid those names on my heart, I received an email from a former high school teacher informing me that this very woman who was a women's ministry leader actually attended his church and had shared with him that she felt led to reach out to me. He was wondering if he could give her my contact information. I was shocked. As if that wasn't enough confirmation that I was to reach out and entrust these women, the wife of my husband's best friend from high school dropped by one day to bring us our shirts for an upcoming charity walk. She told me she was having a tough day, as a result I unexpectedly began sharing what was going on in our home. She just held me, and we cried together. Needless to say, shortly after that day, I contacted those three women, and before long, they were gathered in my home. That was one of the most crucial moments of my journey and truly a turning point—in complete humility, being raw with those I could trust, seeking their wisdom and prayer for our family, and letting them in fully and completely to come alongside of me. Little did I realize that these women would become a source of strength for years to come.

Reflect on your list from the previous chapter. Who do you have to circle the wagons around you when going through tough times? My friend, as we discussed, you do not have to walk your path alone. Seek accountability in your life. Ecclesiastes 4:9-12 reminds us there is strength in numbers. Pray together. James 5:16 tells of the benefits of prayer and sharing struggles with each other. Seek help from counselors, Bible studies, small groups, support groups, whatever resources may be available to you, but you do not have to walk the path alone.

Not sure who to ask or where to seek help? Ask for the wisdom using my dad's ABC tip:

A: ask, according to James 1:5
"If any of you lacks wisdom, you should ask God, who gives generously to all without finding fault, and it will be given to you."
B: believe God will answer and provide, as in James 1:6
"But when you ask, you must believe and not doubt, because the one who doubts is like a wave of the sea, blown and tossed by the wind."
C: commit to it, as in Proverbs 3:5-6
"Trust in the Lord with all your heart and lean not on your own understanding; in all your ways submit to him, and he will make your paths straight."

That year of separation for us led to multiple counselors, dozens of books, much prayer, countless tears, and many restless nights. I had even begun personally seeing a counselor every week. My heart sank when I finally heard those dreaded words come from my husband's mouth—the ones I didn't believe should exist within a Christian marriage, let alone our marriage—"I want a divorce."

I'll never forget the day we met to sign the divorce papers. Pleading for our marriage one last time before the stroke of the pen was made, and we were done. As I walked out the door, I got in my car and wept. As I turned on the car, God once again lifted my head as I heard the song "Promises" by Sanctus Real playing on the radio.[8] Its lyrics remind us that God works everything for our good, so no matter what we are going through in life, He can bring healing, strength, and love as He assures us that He keeps His promises to us. We just have to cling to those promises—the promises of God.

In the coming months, for one reason or another, the divorce papers weren't going through, and I praised God, thanking Him for more time for my marriage to be saved. I did the *Love Dare*[9] (a forty-day challenge by Stephen and Alex McKendrick to understand and practice unconditional love on your spouse), prayed, gave special gifts of encouragement to my husband, reflected on personal areas for which I needed to seek forgiveness, and sent text messages of care to him. I pleaded with God to work a miracle. Then that day came. I received the call, "Holly, congratulations! You are divorced." The legal clerk didn't understand my lack of enthusiasm as I replied, "There is NOTHING to celebrate. Satan just won my marriage." I realized the full extent that Satan had made his way in through the crevice of temptations. I was reminded that we cannot control other people's choices—only our own. I vowed Satan would never win me, and I committed to God to take this and use it for His glory.

Satan continued to attack in those months following the divorce. Just three months after the divorce, I received a call from my boss (I worked from home as an event director for a local chamber), asking to meet with him in his office. As I sat in the uncomfortable wobble-legged chair across from him and beside a well-dressed board member, my boss tried to explain that the budget was tight, and cutbacks were needed to make ends meet. With only four of us employed by the chamber, and me being the last one hired five years prior, I was the one being cut. Divorced, a single mom, and now unemployed. As if the weight of the world didn't already press heavily upon my shoulders, this would be followed by the dishwasher breaking, the microwave dying, the dryer seeing its final days, the roof needing to be replaced, the water heater in dire straits, the HVAC going out, finding mold in old window seals, the fence falling over and needing to be replaced, and too many bills mounted on the counter. All I could do was hang my head, close my eyes, and cling to God's promises that He would always meet my needs (Philippians 4:19) and trust in His word to:

~

"not be anxious about anything, but in every situation, by prayer and petition, with thanksgiving, present your requests to God"

PHILIPPIANS 4:6

Although officially divorced, I did not feel that God had released me from my vows to my husband. I continued to leave the front porch light on in case my former husband returned home. I couldn't fathom what that would look like, but I trusted God that whatever He might bring me to, He'd walk me through.

A little over a year had passed, and I learned that my husband had gotten remarried. A friend of ours from high school reached out and spoke truth to my heart. She said, "Holly, your big D doesn't stand for divorced, it stands for you being delivered." I once again felt as if the Lord had graciously reached down and lifted my face while saying, "You survived the heartache. Now let's walk through the path of forgiveness together so you may truly be free."

Forgiveness. A word that can bring us to our knees, and yet

is a directive from the Lord in Matthew 6:14-15. Forgiveness is not for the other person, it's for us. Forgiveness allows us the freedom from carrying around the heaviness of the burden, the shame, the anger, the resentment, and help prevent the bitterness from taking root. It does not let the accuser off the hook, justify it, or minimize the offense done to us. It does not renew the relationship, as it may be best for boundaries to be made and put in place, but forgiveness does allow us to be free.

Do you have someone in your life you need to forgive? As Romans 5:3-5 reminds us,

---

"Not only so, but we also glory in our sufferings, because we know that suffering produces perseverance; perseverance, character; and character, hope. And hope does not put us to shame, because God's love has been poured out into our hearts through the Holy Spirit, who has been given to us."

What's preventing you from forgiving the one who has wronged you? Our feelings will often be the last on board with this forgiveness, but God can do something mighty out of this heartache. Oh, if we will but only trust that God has purpose in our path, even in our pain. He can take our heartache and turn it into something beautiful (Isaiah 61:3), but we must let go and let God. Won't you join me in holding onto His promises instead of holding onto the injustices? Forgive—and choose to live free.

Face-Lift Action Step #4

HOW DO WE know if there is something or someone in which we need to forgive? Well, what crosses your mind often? What gets under your skin? What angers you with a simple thought? Is there someone who's presence makes you boil? That's probably a good indication of something or someone to forgive.

Lysa Terkeurst wrote a powerful book called *Forgiving What You Can't Forget.* I highly recommend it and would invite you now to pray this prayer from her book:

> "God I give this situation to You. I release my evidence of all the reasons they were so wrong. I release my need to see this person punished. I release my need for an apology. I release my need for this to feel fair. I release my need for You to declare me right and them wrong. Show me what I need to learn from all of this. And then give me Your peace in place of my anger."
> Amen."[10]

You may need to tab this page, highlight it, or rip it out and hang it up on your bathroom mirror to pray aloud daily—again and again. Forgiveness is rarely immediate; it takes time. All too often, even that one offense might lead to more situational consequences down the road that we'll need to forgive. But not only can God use what Satan meant to harm us and turn it for our good (Genesis 50:20), He can also use it so that the works of God might be displayed in us (John 9:3). Forgiveness also doesn't mean reconciliation. Boundaries may need to be set for your protection. But let go, my friend, and let God. Today, won't you choose to take that first step to forgive?

Holly Harding Curby
April 13, 2013

Are you willing to take the "Love Dare?" - never leave your partner behind. If only more people remembered that their vows were promises not only to their spouse, but to God. Worth the watch...

Face-Lift #4

Heartache Is Painful—
He Will See You Through
And Provide For Your Every Need

"See, I am doing a new thing! Now it springs
up; do you not perceive it?
I am making a way in the wilderness and
streams in the wasteland."

—ISAIAH 43:19

Chapter 5

Poison Leads to Forgiveness

IT WAS A Sunday afternoon, which typically meant lunch at a local restaurant with my family after church. This Sunday, however, with my kids at their dad's, I just felt like heading home, kicking off my high heels, and getting a nap in before they returned from their weekend. I had just walked in the door when the phone rang. Little did I realize, answering that phone would be the beginning of time standing still for the next several weeks.

As I picked up the phone, I heard my dad say, with a panic in his voice, "Your mother thinks she just drank acid. We are on our way to the hospital." I honestly don't recall what I did after that, nor do I recall even driving over to the hospital. I just remember one thing . . . the overwhelming desire to get to my mom—and fast.

As I walked into her room in the emergency room, she was sitting on the side of the bed, spitting into a plastic container. The doctor seemed perplexed as he examined her, unsure what exactly to look for, yet he seemed to think there was something else going on. I must have looked a little puzzled, too, because my dad began to explain what happened. As he was returning from the restroom at a local restaurant, my mom filled up her cup with sweet tea. Being the tea connoisseur that she is, she always has a habit of taking a little sip through the straw to test the sweetness before deciding to add sweetener. As she took the first sip, however, her mouth began to burn, and she quickly spit it out. As Dad relayed the story, the doctor looked over at the cup of tea my dad wisely brought to the emergency room. As the doctor touched the cup to examine it, some of the tea splashed down the side of the cup and touched the doctor's finger. He pulled back in pain as the tea burned through his glove on his skin. He quickly ordered for the tea to be tested with a litmus strip, and the results were off the charts with alkaline. The doctor looked at my mom in complete bewilderment and confirmed, "That is in comparison to you drinking battery acid, but with high alkaline levels." We all were in shock . . . other than a swollen tongue and some canker-like sores on Mom's cheeks, she seemed fine. But our world was about to take quite a turn.

After the doctors and nurses left the room, my mom, Dad, and I chitchatted while we waited for my brother to arrive. Just as he got there, my dad began filling him in on the day's events. Then, suddenly, the doctor came back in the room accompanied by a few medical team members. The room grew quiet upon seeing the deep concern expressed in their eyes. Things were about to get worse. They briefly shared a summary of a phone call they had with the leading doctor from the University of Utah Hospital's burn unit. The doctor explained that the medical team was there to take Mom to another room, where they would intubate her, and then life-flight her to the ICU miles away. The next thing we knew, we were following her bed to another room, nurses placed chairs behind us trying to ensure that we remained calm while watching Mom being intubated. I had been keeping my sister, who was on her way home from a weekend trip with her husband and sons, in the loop via cell phone, but all of this seemed to be happening so quickly. So, I called and told her, "They are putting a breathing tube in Mom and life flighting her to the University of Utah hospital. . . . Tell her you love her, Christy, . . . Talk to her." I still have that image embedded in my mind—my brother, Dad, and I gathered together with my sister on the phone, watching my mom lie there in the bed with a machine breathing for her. Next thing we knew, we were telling my dad to get on the helicopter with my mom and that we'd meet him at the hospital. . . . And just like that, my brother and I stood helplessly as we watched my mom and dad take off in the life flight helicopter.

From a young age, our parents always taught us to pray for others. When we heard an ambulance, they told us to stop and pray for those being taken away. When we saw police directing traffic after a car accident, we would pray for those involved in that crash. When we heard and saw life flight flying overhead, we stopped and prayed for the ones in critical condition. Here I stood, standing next to my six-foot-four brother who towered over me, feeling helpless as we watched life flight take off and fade into the distance of the afternoon sky. We knew it was our parents onboard that we were praying for this time.

Once again, I don't recall how I got to the other hospital, or even if I drove myself or rode with my brother. I do recall walking into that ICU and feeling the sense of extreme urgency and empathy from the staff as they let us through the locked doors. We finally came down the hall leading to my mom's room, and there was my dad standing outside her room, relieved to see us. He shared with us how scary it was to arrive at the hospital and find eight gowned, masked, and gloved doctors and nurses awaiting Mom's arrival, how terrifying when they quickly hooked her up to several machines and asked him to wait outside. It was all too much when the doctor came out to tell us that Mom was in a coma, and their next step was a peripherally inserted central catheter (known as a PICC line).

Then, for a moment, we had peace and a sense of comfort, when the technician who would insert the tube in my mother's heart was a familiar face. We didn't know him well, but he was a gentleman from our church. With a compassionate smile and tone, he assured us that Mom was in good hands, and he proceeded to enter the room with his machine and close the door.

That fellow church member was our angel on earth that day, and the PICC line was a success. The following days brought fears of a perforated esophagus, or fluid gathering around her lungs and heart, or the fact that she was still in a coma, a machine breathing for her. From the beginning, doctors told us that she might not make it, and even if she did, she'd never be the same—perhaps an ostomy bag, her speech gone, or other issues.

Media picked up on Mom's story, and before long, we heard of people not only across the nation but across the world praying for my mom. People both known and unknown would send cards, which we posted on Mom's hospital room wall to see when she awoke. Balloons and flowers were sent as well. Others visited us to pray, sit in the lobby, and even bring food for us, as we weren't leaving the hospital in hopes of being there when she woke up. They also offered to pick up our kids or even entertain them in the hospital. The love and support was overwhelming. We saw God answer our prayers and work miracles. No, we didn't understand this, but we trusted that although we may not know what the next step would be, we did know that God would guide each and every step along the way.

Nearly a week later, that miraculous moment arrived when

Mom woke up. We smiled, we cried, and we tried to help her remain calm by explaining what was happening, then she looked at her grandchildren and her family gathered around her bedside and smiled. The doctors continued to tell us we weren't out of the woods yet, but we saw God at work. Coming off the ventilator, taking her first steps, test after test revealing encouraging news instead of major damage, and even hearing her whisper after much time of silence—yes, God was most definitely in this, and we gave thanks.

My dad once shared in a message, "In times of trials, it's what you do next that reveals your true faith." I was humbled by seeing my family respond during this time. My brother was so inspirational as he put encouraging quotes in her room, getting right up next to her bedside, holding her hand, and reminding her she is strong, and she's got this. My sister so tenderly helped care for my mom and meet each need that arose. My dad, ever so faithful and by her bedside, held her hand and told her how proud he was of her and how very much he loved her. My brother-in-law became her "security" with visitors as he tried to help my mother keep her dignity during one of the toughest times of her life. And even my soon-to-be sister-in-law would patiently wait in the lobby, acting as a host for when visitors came. During this time, I reflected upon Romans 8:18 that says,

"I consider that our present sufferings are not worth comparing with the glory that will be revealed in us."

God will never bring us to something that He can't bring us through, and bring us through as a family, He did.

During this time, media attention grew more and more, and as I turned to the outlet of social media to update family and friends, my dad and brother were common faces on the news. Again and again, the media inquired about anger toward the company that caused this through their negligence. Time and time again, my dad would so graciously reply that "one of our hopes is that something good can come out of something tragic." Just as Dad had preached from the pulpit that "one life will soon be passed. Only what's done for Christ will last," Dad used this media attention to share His faith and declare what would become our family motto—"God's got us."

Not wanting family and friends to have to follow the news to be updated about Mom's condition, I began using my Facebook presence as a more personal way to keep them in the loop. This was also a perfect avenue to request prayer for whatever challenge laid ahead for that day, to share praises of the miracles we were seeing, and to thank our friends and family for their continued care, love, and support. Mom was also encouraged by the reading of these posts and comments from friends and family. This was truly a fundamental time in learning how impacting social media outlets can be. In a world with such an "everything is fine" façade, we were able to be transparent with our heartache, find comfort in the comments to posts, and somehow provide a sense of comfort to others who were going through their own battles. This was a revelation that social media, while it certainly has its negatives, can actually be used intentionally for positive impacts.

Two weeks following the incident, we began seeing more improvements. Mom passed her swallowing test, had her PICC line removed, was eventually moved out of the ICU into the trauma unit, and had her feeding tube removed. As one of Mom's favorite songs says, each step that we take, God can lead us to where we truly can follow Him each and every day of our life.[11] Each day was providing new steps, and we were grateful for the progress. And finally, the day came as Mark 5:34 declares,

"He said to her, 'Daughter, your faith has healed you.
Go in peace and be freed from your suffering.'"

Yes, Mom got to go home, just in time for her and my dad to celebrate their forty-sixth wedding anniversary that very day.

I must confess, through all of this, although I spent hour upon hour at Mom's bedside playing songs that seemed fitting for the moments, such as Jamie Grace's, "Fighter"[12], reading encouraging posts to Mom from my social media, and even spending time in prayer with those who came by to visit, I, myself, don't recall what I prayed. For some, I may have just lost you, but for others, you can relate with the emptiness you feel, the trauma of what you are living that leaves you paralyzed and speechless. I felt completely weak and empty holding on to hope that my Healer could bring healing if He chose, but I didn't have the words to express my heart. Although I felt that our lives for those two weeks consisted of constant praying (1 Thessalonians 5:16-18), it was Romans 8:26-27 that I felt had been lived out in my life during this time.

"In the same way, the Spirit helps us in our weakness. We do not know what we ought to pray for, but the Spirit himself intercedes for us through wordless groans. And he who searches our hearts knows the mind of the Spirit, because the Spirit intercedes for God's people in accordance with the will of God."

Have you felt that loss for words as you tried to think of what you'd even say when approaching the throne of God through prayer? It's okay. Just as when tucking our children in bed at night, they don't need us to necessarily say anything, they just want our presence of being with them. God desires the same of us—to simply be with Him.

As weeks passed, Mom's body was still in the healing process. She'd want to go exercise, run errands, or just garden, but her body would quickly remind her of the still partially collapsed lung, the muscle fatigue, and that she was still not feeling like herself yet. The emotional, physical, and mental toll of the weeks in ICU caught up with our family, too. From migraine headaches and illnesses to complete exhaustion, each of our family members was affected in one way or another. Satan seemed to be on the attack. It was about that time that the media requested a final interview with our family, and out of exhaustion, we just weren't sure we had anything left to offer. Have you ever been to that point? Perhaps you are there now. You just don't feel like you have anything left to give. You are tired, worn, heavy-laden, and perhaps waving your white flag in complete surrender. As the poem, "Footprints in the Sand," concludes, "When you saw only one set of footprints, it was then that I carried you."[13] He will carry you, my friend. You can and will get through this, one step at a time.

As we gathered at the press conference, our family prayed for God to renew our strength, for Him to have all glory, and that we would not be a stumbling block. We asked God to reflect His light in our lives so that, as Toby Mac sings in one of his songs, God could "steal the show."[14] The next hour was stretched out with questions for Mom, such as what she remembered or experienced, her medical care received, and even about how she felt toward the restaurant who caused this scare. Mom shared that there were times she did not believe she would survive, but that she had asked God to send an angel because the journey felt too hard. She told news reporters that she never saw an angel. As to the doctors, she gave high compliments and thanked them for their care. As to the restaurant, she said that it wasn't in her nature to be vengeful, rather she just hoped that the restaurant would take steps to ensure this would not happen to anyone else, ever again.

Revenge. How often in our human nature do we want to see justice served? But we are instructed in Romans 12:19-21,

"Do not take revenge, my dear friends, but leave room for God's wrath, for it is written: "It is mine to avenge; I will repay," says the Lord. On the contrary: "If your enemy is hungry, feed him; if he is thirsty, give him something to drink. In doing this, you will heap burning coals on his head." Do not be overcome by evil, but overcome evil with good."

That goodness, God's goodness, is exactly what we focused on. That next year would involve many follow-up doctor appointments for Mom. One doctor even shared that he wouldn't be surprised if something surfaced five years from now. We chose to focus on the blessings of God's goodness and not worry about the unknowns, trusting those to God. After all, we had just lived through Deuteronomy 31:8:

"The Lord himself goes before you and will be with you; he will never leave you nor forsake you. Do not be afraid; do not be discouraged."

To the community's amazement, no lawsuit was ever filed, but rather a common reminder that Mom's recovery was credited to God and God alone. Our family was even able to meet the restaurant's franchise owner. One by one, we went up to shake his hand or give him a hug of compassion as we assured him, "We forgive you."

As a survivor, Mom spoke at women's events, accepted phone calls, responded to letters from people across the nation seeking the hope she had to apply to their own trials in life, and shared testimony during Bible Studies. We don't always get to choose what happens to us in life, but we do get to choose how it shapes us, how we grow from it, thrive from it, and use it. Just as my mom was living out Genesis 50:20,

———⸱◞

"You [Satan] intended to harm me, but God intended it for good to accomplish what is now being done, the saving of many lives."

Oh, dear loved one, He can do the same for you.

Face-Lift Action Step #5

JUST AS MY mom took what she had been through and used her experience to help others, you can take your story and use it to encourage, inspire, and equip those around you. After all, inspired people inspire people.

The following is a list on ways you can use your journey in life to help others:

- Speaking Engagements
- Social Media/Blog
- Send Letters/Cards
- Become A Non-Profit Ambassador
- Become An Advocate
- Mentor Others
- Research
- Volunteer Time or Money
- Podcast/Media Interview
- Join/Lead A Support Group
- Meet for Coffee
- Journal
- Empathize/Show Compassion
- Become Someone's Prayer Warrior

Look at your story timeline from chapter 1 and your challenges from chapter 2. What are some ways you can use your story to help others?

_____

_____

_____

_____

_____

_____

_____

_____

_____

_____

What is one way you'll start using your story today?

_____

_____

_____

_____

_____

_____

_____

_____

_____

_____

Holly Harding Curby
August 17, 2014

Exhaustion is completely setting in and yet we raise our voices to God in praise at His mercies that are new every morning. This morning was a GREAT morning for mom...she was able to whisper a little louder (although not her voice as her larynx is burnt), she walked around the unit floor once, she put forth much effort in therapy and she and I were able to join in worship via FaceTime as my dad celebrated his 50th year anniversary of his first time preaching (again, thank you to all the friends who attended to support my family who was there and specifically my dad!). What a blessed morning.

And yet, with that said, mom is still listed in critical condition and the doctors do still say she is "not out of the woods yet". The damage done internally to her esophagus is severe. These next two days she will work on therapy and rest as she prepares for another procedure (endoscopy) on Wednesday to check on the status of the damage. Each day brings forth some new trials and therefore more opportunities to take our concerns to the foot of the cross.

So, how can you pray tonight? FIRST: Please pray for complete rest for mom. Rest mentally from her thoughts. Rest physically from the demands of the day. Rest emotionally as this trial takes it's toll on her. We keep thanking her for fighting and giving her little "pep talks". She is amazing and truly our hero!! SECOND: That her esophagus will not perforate as the burns are deep and go into the chest cavity of the esophagus and have many lesions on them. This is one major factor that they watch daily and impacts her condition greatly! THIRD: For overall provision and protection and renewal of/for our family. So many things go into this...

God knows the concerns of our hearts and our limits. I am so blessed with such a strong family who remains unified in Him and with one another. I am overwhelmed at my love for my dad, brother and sister, and that I can't ease life that still pulls on each of us during such a tragic time. God's got us....our faith is in Him and Him alone! We conclude today with a reminder from Romans 8:18, "I consider that our present sufferings are not worth comparing with the glory that will be revealed in us." God will never bring us to something that He can't bring us through. To God alone be the glory, to God alone be the praise! Praising you God for a new day with blessings to show us you've got this...

Face-Lift #5

Poison Leads to Forgiveness—
He Will Protect You

"I lift up my eyes up to the mountains—where
does my help comes from?
My help comes from the Lord, the Maker of
heaven and earth."

—PSALM 121:1-2

Chapter 6

Cancer Is Devastating

IT WAS A beautiful spring afternoon. The birds were chirping and the flowers were blooming. My sister, brother-in-law, brother, and I had gathered at my brother's house to pray prior to going to my parents' house for a "family meeting." We weren't sure what was going on, but we all had the same vibe—and it wasn't good. We committed to have a positive attitude and focus on Mom and Dad in whatever they had to share.

At the house, my dad began to explain that he had been feeling a little weak for a few weeks. Each day of his workout, he was unable to do as many pushups as he had before. He had a bit of a cough, but nothing of concern, and had lost a little weight without explanation. So, at his next physical, he shared these observations with our family doctor, not putting much thought into them. The results, as he had learned and was now telling us, were those dreaded words that most fear hearing, "It's cancer." The doctor went to the lab personally to confirm the diagnosis. Honestly, I think the only thing my siblings and I heard was white noise. As I looked across the room, I saw my brother in one chair and my sister in another with faces of complete shock, disbelief, and emotion. I, the youngest of the three kids, suddenly felt it was my job to comfort and protect them, but I didn't know how. This news didn't have a face to be angry at and didn't have a presence to walk away from, so I did the only thing I knew to do. I went over, knelt in between them, and just held them. Inside I felt full of rage as my soul cried out, "Why, God? Not my dad, not the patriarch of our family!"

Have you ever felt angry at God? Perhaps your situation or life circumstances have had you wondering where His goodness is, or where His protection upon you and/or your family was in a certain moment. Maybe a prayer wasn't answered in the way you felt it should have been. Or maybe you just haven't felt his presence in a long time. And, of course, there is the all-too-familiar anger at God when questioning, if He is so good, then why did this or that happen in your life? You may be surprised to hear that even God experienced this emotion of anger (Matthew 21:12-13), and even people in the Bible got angry at God (check out the story of Jeremiah in Jeremiah 20:7-10 or even David's cry in Psalm 22:1). The concern is when anger gives way for Satan to have a foothold in your life (Ephesians 4:26-27), which can open up a destructive path, including bitterness and resentment.

My dad, being the true man of God that he is, shared with us that he considered this trial to be one that God entrusted him to go through to both represent and share his faith. After all, as dad has often said, "If I could fully understand or explain God to you, why would I worship Him?" We committed that day as a family to continue to live out Joshua 24:15b that says,

~9

"But as for me and my household,
we will serve the Lord."

As days passed, my sister, Mom, and I decided to proceed with our preplanned weekend trip back to Missouri to help a family friend whose wife had recently been diagnosed with Alzheimer's. We were awaiting the results of Dad's recent tests, which would indicate the stage of the cancer and therefore allow a treatment plan to be put in place. Dad was driving us to the airport when we got the call. "Stage 4, multiple myeloma." The news was not good, and the doctor told us to immediately drive to the hospital so that my dad could be admitted.

That weekend took a different turn, for sure. Dad was in the hospital for days, and during that time, we, as a family, took education classes to learn how to feed, care, and protect Dad. Although multiple myeloma is incurable, gratefully, it is treatable, so we were entering a long road ahead of us. Chemotherapy, infusions, labs, and bone marrow biopsies quickly became a new regimen for Dad.

With Dad's weakened immune system, he was susceptible to anything and everything. Just months after his diagnosis, we found ourselves rushing him to the Huntsman Cancer Hospital acute care only to learn that Dad had become septic. After a fever peak of 105.8, doctors were able to finally stabilize him. It was scary, and the doctor told my mom that he basically had a fifty-fifty chance of surviving. In addition, this new development was going to delay Dad's bone marrow transplant. With exhaustion from the on-the-edge-of-your-seat days, trying to get the fever down, and now the unknown of the timeline for procedures that lay ahead, we found ourselves trusting in Isaiah 40:31 that says,

"But those who hope in the Lord will renew their strength. They will soar on wings like eagles; they will run and not grow weary, they will walk and not be faint."

Once again, in the midst of such trials, we used my Facebook page as a way to simplify the process of keeping family and friends updated on Dad's status. Once again, family and friends were the ones encouraging us through their comments of care and concern. Now, I will be the first to admit that I'd rather invite friends and family over to my home, where we can sit on the back deck and enjoy the presence of each other's company, but in times where many were reaching out and we had limited time to keep all informed, social media was so valuable. There is something to be said for those late-night hours of solitude, where you can log in and read comments and direct messages of hope, encouragement, and even people reflecting on fond memories of your loved one. You suddenly don't feel so alone.

As we stayed by Dad's bedside, watching this strong man fight for his life, it was hard to comprehend how this year had turned. We had started out with the news that I needed major hip surgery. As mentioned in the first chapter, I had been diagnosed with Legg-Calve-Perthes disease as a child and underwent traction treatment. Doctors told my parents that I would need a hip replacement at about forty years old. Well, I was five years shy of that age, but my friend (who was also our family physician and attended a women's weekly Bible study in my home) noticed my limping and constant pain in my hip while I was training for a half marathon. She advised me to have it looked at, and as a result, it was discovered that there was some work to be done, reshaping my hip bone and some clean-up of the ligaments and tendons. What was said to be a week or two at most on bedrest ended up being close to six or eight weeks. Although the surgery was a success, my hip flexor muscle wasn't healing as hoped. I was unable to drive for twelve weeks, not allowed to wear heels for close to six months, and required an entire year of physical therapy.

My children and I temporarily moved in with my brother so I could avoid stairs (he had a spare bedroom and bathroom just off the kitchen and a family room on the main level). My parents helped shuttle my children to and from school, my mom helped my children with their homework and even chaperoned my daughter's field trip to the zoo in the snow, my sister and some church friends helped provide meals, and it was my dad who tended to me at all hours of the night as I had to keep an ice pack machine on my hip twenty-four hours a day, seven days a week. That man, who would set his alarm clock for the middle of the night to change my ice, the man who took me to all of my follow-up doctor's visits, was now laying there, weak and in pain, fighting for his life. I felt helpless, as there was nothing I could do to help him as he had helped me.

The bone marrow transplant process was going to take thirty days. The first fourteen days of that timeframe, our family decided to provide encouragement by each member adopting a day to do something special. One young nephew spent his own money to build a teddy bear at a local build-your-own-stuffed-animal store. Another had a football signed by our family and my dad's closest friends. My sister created a playlist of some of Dad's favorite songs and then downloaded them to his Kindle to listen to during his treatments. I had compiled a collection of nearly seventy audio messages from Dad's friends and colleagues from throughout the years with encouraging words and/or favorite memories with Dad. One of my kids did a homemade pillowcase, and so forth. Our goal was to lift Dad's spirits and remind him of his support team, As a family, through his fight, we each wore a bracelet that read,

———ᵕ⁹

"I can do all this through him who gives me strength"

PHILIPPIANS 4:13.

Perhaps you know of someone going through their own battle, and you don't know how to help them, you've never experienced the trial they are facing, and you don't have the words to say. My friend, you don't need only words to encourage.

My mom used to co-teach a women's Bible study at church and speak at various women's events. I recall one of her lessons focusing on ways we can encourage others. My mom used to refer to them as the "Bee Garden" and would even use an image of a bee to help them visually stick in the ladies' minds.

1. **BEE LOVINGLY BOLD.**

   My mom taught me and my siblings from a young age to seek out those in a room who didn't seem to fit in or feel a part of what was going on; do something, whether it's going over and initiating conversation, inviting them into the activity, or simply sitting or standing next to them. Try to draw others out —don't let them just hunker down alone. Look around you to see who needs a little encouragement.

2. **BEE COMMITTED.**

   As the saying goes, everyone is going through a battle you know nothing about. Remember some life wounds (divorce, family deaths, cancers) don't heal in two weeks. Look for ways to encourage and meet ongoing needs.

3. **BEE UPLIFTING.**

I remember when I went through my divorce, a lady asked me to come out to her car because she had something for me. She handed me a jar of fancy food, and with a look of pity on her face, she proceeded to tell me she heard I was going through a rough time, so she wanted to give me these. Oh, friends, when helping others, try to give them a hand up (encouragement, treat as equals), not just a handout. By doing so, you help them stand firm with dignity and strength to face each day—not embarrassment, shame, or degradation for what they are going through. Me and my kids love to do secret cupid and secret Santa. So, every Valentine's Day we choose people from our walks of life (school, church, neighborhood, work) who could use some loving. We then get a treat and a card and go "doorbell ditch" them with our anonymous gift. Same with Christmas, we get Christmas gifts, wrap them, and go doorbell ditch individuals, families, couples, or whomever we feel could use a little encouragement. Why? I know how it feels to be on the opposite end. I don't want anyone to feel indebted, embarrassed, or ashamed. I just want them to feel loved, to be encouraged, and to have a lifting of their head.

4. **BEE GENUINE.**

Much like uplifting above, we want to make sure our motives for encouraging others are not of selfish gain (although, don't get me wrong, when we are serving others, I gotta tell ya, we are blessed too). Whether it is something they teach us (I remember serving Thanksgiving meals to the homeless under the Viaduct with my family as a little girl and an older man giving me a little teddy bear he had carried around. I learned so much humility that day and a new perspective of being grateful for what I had) or something we learn (when doing Habitat For Humanity, I felt so humbled hearing the story of the woman moving into the house), serving others has a way of being good for our soul. But we must focus on serving with the intent of genuinely bringing encouragement to the one we are loving. One of my favorite experiences in trying to get this point across to my son was when he was in Primary Children's Hospital a couple of years ago. We went down to the cafeteria for breakfast together and paid the cashier a certain amount, instructing that the money go toward a patient and their family (each parent of a kid being treated had certain stickers to wear at the hospital), and to say, "Your bill is taken care of," and "have a nice day." My son couldn't understand why we weren't telling people it was us. I told him, "What's our point in doing this? To receive acknowledgment for the act, or to encourage others going through rough times?" Of course, he said the latter, so we sat there for a good hour and watched the faces of the parents as they were told their meal had been paid for. Do you know what I noticed? Not only the smiles on their faces but the smile and pure delight and joy on my son's face as he watched family after family leave the cash register. Be genuine. Encourage to encourage.

5. **BEE CREATIVE.**

Encouraging others isn't a cookie-cutter act. As I shared before, when I was six years old, I developed a hip problem and had to be in twenty-four-hour, seven-day-a-week traction. At the same time, my brother had to undergo major kidney surgery, and both my traction and his surgery were beginning on the same day. My sister was quite a trooper in helping me while my parents were juggling time at the hospital with my brother, but I think she was quite relieved when ladies from our church heard what our family was going through, and one woman and her son came dressed in clown costumes to entertain me, another lady came and helped me with my homework, and others brought food. A few years ago, I had to have hip surgery for this very same hip problem, and one woman from our current church came with a wheelchair once a week and took me on a walk around the neighborhood (being on bedrest for like six weeks, other than going to physical therapy, this was the only time I got to be outside). The "herd" ministered to us in many creative ways.

6. **BEE OPEN.**

A zebra herd needs to be willing to overcome age boundaries. When my mom was a young pastor's wife, the older ladies taught her to can, garden, and sew. She used those skills to can for our family, share her bountiful garden with neighbors, and sew hundreds of robes for breast cancer patients at Huntsman Cancer Institute. Likewise, her and my dad are not, should we call them, "techies." So, they have had to rely on younger people like my daughter to help them do things. We all need each other and have something to offer the older and the younger. My mom has always encouraged me to have a mentor, someone older and wiser who has experienced enough life that they can share their wisdom with me, but also to be a mentor to others.

7. **BEE RECEPTIVE.**

Now this is probably one of the most difficult for most of us. Just as we try to encourage others, we have got to be open ourselves to receiving encouragement from others. I've gone through some trying times in my life, as I'm sure you have too, and accepting help is not easy. I personally feel like I'm inconveniencing people, or that I'll be "indebted" to them. I know that sounds crazy. But I also learned from a Sunday school teacher not to rob others of the joy of blessing you. I've seen this when my mom drank poisonous tea and laid in a coma in the ICU, when my dad was diagnosed with blood cancer, and many more times yet to be discussed in this book. Our waiting room filled with people from throughout our lifetime coming to pray with us, provide meals to us right there in the hospital, and get our kids to their activities (one thoughtful woman even bought a first day of school outfit for my son one year, as she knew I had no time to do back to school shopping). Kids my mom used to teach came and pulled weeds in their yard, neighbors mowed our yards, and many brought meals, knowing our attentions and energies were spoken for with a million other tasks and needs of the day. It's so hard to accept help, but it's one area of life where we must have humility and simply reply with a "thank you."

Whether giving your time, supporting a cause, donating financially, or simply finding your creative way to encourage another, just remember that it is often our actions that speak much louder than anything else. As they say, it truly is the thought that counts.

As we strived to implement all of these in encouraging my dad, he continued to put his faith and trust in God. He reflected once during the bone marrow transplant that this had been the most difficult challenge he'd faced in his life. That statement was coming from someone who has served our country through his service in the Air Force and was even deployed during the Vietnam War. Severe pain, minimal hours of sleep, medical challenges, changes in symptoms, the loss of strength and energy, the unsteadiness of balance which sometimes required him to walk with a cane, the impact on his body from months of subjection to a number of very powerful drugs, and the surgical implantation of a device in his chest through which the medical professionals drew blood and did infusions, all became a part of his regular battles. Yet, he'd always say, "God has allowed this into my life because He has a plan for using it in a very special way. Therefore, I feel honored that He would choose me for such a mission and in such a way. The Lord has always been faithful to His people, and this has certainly been true in my life." He'd continue that he had the greatest confidence in God and His continued provision throughout this time and that the Lord was and would continue to use it to teach him, make him stronger, and to make him more useful to Him in the future. I can honestly say, watching my dad go through this inspired me. He was humble, wise, drew upon the strength of the Lord, and truly was a faithful servant (Matthew 25:21).

Eight months after diagnosis, following chemotherapy, bone marrow biopsies, and a transplant, we received the good news from the doctor that the treatment was a success, and Dad's cancer was officially in remission. Doctors not only reported that things couldn't have gone any better, but they were puzzled as to why Dad's fight against an incurable disease proved some scientific theories wrong. It felt very much like when Mom went through the poisoned tea incident the year prior, how doctors had said there was no way on earth she shouldn't have permanent damage at best. Faith of a mustard seed (Matthew 17:20) and a living God who still performs miracles. Dad would now need to start a maintenance plan of meds for the three years to come, he would still suffer with permanent neuropathy in his feet, which is quite painful, and he was forewarned that multiple myeloma usually returns after a few years at most, but Dad had fought the good fight, and he won.

Through the pain, fear, and damage that cancer did, we were encouraged by "What Cancer Cannot Do," written by an unknown author.

Cancer is so limited . . .
It cannot cripple Love.
It cannot shatter Hope.
It cannot corrode Faith.
It cannot destroy Peace.
It cannot kill Friendship.
It cannot suppress Memories.
It cannot invade the Soul.
It cannot steal Eternal Life.
It cannot conquer The Spirit.[15]

Dad never quit, he fought hard, and his trust never wavered:

"But let all who take refuge in you be glad; let them ever sing for joy. Spread your protection over them, that those who love your name may rejoice in you. Surely, Lord, you bless the righteous; you surround them with your favor as with a shield."

PSALM 5:11-12.

As we left the hospital that day, after learning of Dad's remission, the skies crystal clear and the sun shining brightly above, a gentle breeze swept across our faces as, once again, we felt the Lord lift our face and say, "I've got you."

Face-Lift Action Step #6

IN TIMES OF weariness, we can become a recluse, wallow in self-pity, or even seek out others in despair as misery seems to love company, but there is a different approach we can take. In the midst of our season, we can look outside ourselves for someone to encourage, serve, or simply show care for. My mom lived by the motto, "Be the reason someone smiles today." Below are ways we can encourage others:

- Mow their yard so they can care for a loved one.
- Provide a meal so it's one less thing on their to-do list.
- Write them a card/letter telling them you are thinking of them.
- Put together a care package to leave at their front doorstep.
- Take them out for coffee, & simply listen to them/sit in silence.
- Provide a meaningful gift (picture frame, décor plaque).
- Provide gift cards to eateries for their family to eat out.
- Give them sporting/entertainment tickets to have a distraction.
- Offer your second home or camper for them to go away together.
- Provide transportation to their medical visits.

- Offer to sit in the waiting room with them.

- Contact their utility company to pay a utility bill (unless they rent, then this may not reach them).

What are some ways people have positively and effectively encouraged you during tough seasons in life?

_____

_____

_____

_____

_____

_____

_____

Who will you seek to serve and be the reason they smile this week? And how?

_____

_____

_____

_____

_____

_____

_____

Holly Harding Curby
September 27, 2015

Update on dad (Jim Harding) : well prayer warriors....we are approaching the crucial period in dad's battle of multiple myeloma. I had many ask about him today at church (thank you!!) so here it goes... He goes in Oct 2 for another bone biopsy. He meets with his cancer Dr Oct 7 to decide what "option" they have decided on for the bone marrow transplant and he has a port installed Oct 9. From there the Dr will test dad's "counts" daily to know when to harvest his stem cells and then shortly after that he has his bone marrow transplant. So these next three to four weeks are crucial. As a few asked today about what they can do: 1) pray for dad's body to stay "healthy" as a cold or flu could jeopardize timing/schedule as well as his condition overall 2) pray for dad's strength, fight and overall body as he no longer has "good days" and things will get rougher before better (although this week shows some hope as his body has a week of "rest" before everything starts) 3) pray for dad's pain level to be bareable and treatments to manage the pain he's already experiencing. 4) for ENCOURAGEMENT for both mom (Jan Harding) and dad as well as renewment, rest and that God will take captive their every thought as the days/nights are getting more demanding (we will be sure to read emails and cards to him and display them in his room during this time) and finally 5) that God will continue to open doors of ministry through this trial and that He truly would be glorified through our lives and how we respond during each step and hurdle. We truly are blessed with you all as our dear friends and family who genuinely care for us, take time to pray for us and haven't given up on us through these past few years of family "ministry opportunities". Our hearts go out to those of you fighting your own battles and we would be honored to pray for you too so please let us know how we can be there for you!   Satan tries his best, but as Dad would say "God's got us"... And " in the end, He wins!"

Face-Lift #6

Cancer Is Devastating—
He Is Our Healer

"You intended to harm me,
but God intended it for good to accomplish
what is now being done,
the saving of many lives."

—GENESIS 50:20

Chapter 7

Waging War Is Exhausting

I'LL NEVER FORGET the day I heard the doorbell ring, and I opened the door to an unfamiliar stern face holding out a packet and saying, "Holly Curby? You've been served." And just as quickly as he appeared, he was gone. Living proof that our presence in one's life may be brief but life changing. Opening the papers, I read what would soon lead to the longest three years of my life. The one thing the state advised us never to do during our divorce was go after one another via a custody evaluator.

Although this is only the seventh chapter of the book, it is the one I have prayed over the most. The one that brings about the most pain in what feels like such an evil way. It's the one I have wrestled with the most—what do I share, and what do I NOT share?—as our human tendency is to let others know what people have done to hurt us, yet details don't always bring about good, or even closure, but as I mentioned in chapter 4, they can often distract and be more harmful. Again, that's not the purpose of this book. That wouldn't glorify God. Although I'd prefer omitting this whole chapter altogether, it is a part of my story, and I trust that God is at work in my story, therefore I also choose to trust Him in relinquishing to Him the details, and then using my story as He would.

I will say that it was only by the grace of God, the strength of those prayer warriors once again holding up my arms as Aaron and Hur did for Moses (Exodus 17:12), and a miracle of God that I survived.

As I previously shared, my dad said in a sermon, "In a crisis, what you choose to do next shows you what you believe about God." So, in this crisis, I focused *not* on the person who appeared to be bringing the battle but on the truth of what this was— spiritual warfare. One of my prayer warriors led me to the song "Waging War" by CeCe Winans.[16] This song very quickly became my theme song for this season. Oh, how I would encourage you to hear it in its powerful entirety. It is a battle cry refusing to allow Satan to steal from us. A reminder that our weapon in any battle is our armor of God.

Every morning, I would get up and play this song. Every time I headed to meet with the lawyer, I would play this song. Every time I headed into court, I would play this song. Every time I had to go to meet with the custody evaluator, I would play this song. As I listened to this song, I would picture each piece of God's armor (Ephesians 6:10-17) being put on me. Literally suiting up with each part of my armor:

- The belt of truth, as I asked God to speak truth in the midst of the lies.

- The breastplate of righteousness, as I asked God to help protect my heart and not allow me to sink to the low tactics and attacking words.

- The shoes fit for readiness to stand my ground in not being moved in the cheap shots that would come my way.

- The helmet of salvation, reminding myself who I am in the Lord and that what He called me to, He would equip me for and see me through.

- That shield of faith, trusting in who He says He is and what He says He'll do in Exodus 14:14, "The Lord will fight for you: you need only to be still."

- And finally, that sword of the spirit in my hands. Not to fight with harsh words, insults, and attacks but with the Word of God as my "lamp for my feet, a light on my path" (Psalm 119:105) and refusing to compromise to the world's standards.

Perhaps you can relate with the desire to let others know of the offenses caused to you, or to defend yourself with a sharp tongue. I was in a meeting once where my superior lost his cool in front of a board member. I'll never forget just letting him vent, holding my tongue to lash back, yet once he was finished, I simply asked, "Do you feel better now?" I saw more shame in his eyes of the words he spoke than relief in sharing them. I read once that words are like holes in a fence; once you say them, the damage is done. I have also experienced being disparaged behind my back and, thankfully, of others speaking up for me. Oh, friend, there is a time and place to speak up and stand our ground, but might we take a moment to pray through Ephesians 4:31 before we respond in haste?

"Get rid of all bitterness, rage and anger, brawling
and slander, along with every form of malice."

May our alternative be to suit up. Throughout this battle, the toughest thing I felt I had to do was pray for my former husband. I would reread and meditate on 2 Timothy 2:24-26,

"And the Lord's servant must not be quarrelsome but
must be kind to everyone, able to teach, not resentful.
Opponents must be gently instructed, in the hope
that God will grant them repentance leading them
to a knowledge of the truth, and that they will come
to their senses and escape from the trap of the devil,
who has taken them captive to do his will."

This soon led me to pray for my former husband, asking for his eyes to be open to all the pain this battle was causing so many, asking God's protection for his new wife, that she would never have to go through something like this, and that their child would never be placed in such heartache or have to be raised going back and forth from home to home.

Prayer is both powerful and effective (James 5:16), but most of all, it changes the one praying. During deceitful attacks, it keeps bitterness and resentment from taking root within you. Now please don't misunderstand; I am a sinner saved by grace. I am human. There are times my tongue slipped in attack. There were times my mind didn't think pure thoughts. There are times I still wrestle with forgiveness, and I have to choose often to forgive for continued and/or consequential offenses. I believe this will be an ongoing process, but mandatory of me (Colossians 3:13).

I believe that in trials of life, we have three choices: run/hide from it, fight/grumble our way through it, or choose to grow from it. I absolutely hated this season. It was painful as a former wife to see the coldness in one's eyes, someone you once called your best friend and entrusted with your life. It was heartbreaking as a mom to watch your children have to walk that unwanted path. It was financially breaking to have to pay for something you didn't even want to pursue. It was emotionally draining to have to relive repressed facts, providing them in order to defend yourself from attacks while also seeking wisdom in what to share, but I knew if I had to go through it, I wanted to learn and grow from it. Beth Moore put it well in her Bible study of 1 Samuel[17]—"God always works to prepare us to serve Him, but He rarely prepares us in ways we expect." In 2009, I felt called to women's ministry but didn't see how I could be qualified or effective. I was learning I had to go through a lot of heartbreak to be able to relate more with others, including what it's like to go through the hell of a custody battle. As my dad shared in a sermon once, "Instead of asking God how to get out of this, try asking God what can I get from this?" This perspective helps us look at our trials and challenges as an opportunity to learn and grow.

During this time, I found myself using my social media page to grow out of my comfort zones and remind myself to live life. When I felt discouraged or down, I would look back through my old posts to see God's blessings. Friend, as my dad has told me time and time again, "Don't forget in the dark what God has shown you in the light." Circumstances may have us feeling like we are drowning, all alone, with no end in sight, but we must remember to look for the good in each day. I always ask my children, "Where did you see God today?" Counting our blessings can help turn our perspective around.

I'll never forget the night before our final court date. My dad had pointed me to Habakkuk 3:17-19 which says,

"Though the fig tree does not bud
and there are no grapes on the vines,
though the olive crop fails
and the fields produce no food,
though there are no sheep in the pen
and no cattle in the stalls,
yet I will rejoice in the Lord,
I will be joyful in God my Savior.
The Sovereign Lord is my strength;
He makes my feet like the feet of a deer,
He enables me to go on the heights."

This spoke such peace from God to me, and as our family gathered for prayer at my parents' house, I found myself weeping before the Lord in declaration and complete surrender. "Lord, no matter what happens tomorrow, I will still serve you! I will still worship you! I will still love you! I will still trust you! And I will still follow you! Into your hands, I commit my children."

That next day, I arrived early to prayer walk the halls of the courthouse. I do not believe there were any winners that day, as such battles are scarring, and there is so much damage done along the way. I do believe God showed up. He answered prayers.

"For the revelation awaits an appointed time;
it speaks of the end and will not prove false.
Though it linger, wait for it;
it will certainly come and will not delay"

HABAKKUK 2:3

As I mentioned before, something this tragic doesn't just affect the plaintiff and respondent, it impacts the children, the families, and even the people who know any of the ones involved. During this time, my mom spent many hours on her knees before the throne of God, praying on behalf of me and my children. She shared with me three simple words, yet with such powerful meaning, that she learned through this near three-year battle: seek, surrender, survive. Readers, through whatever trial comes your way, seek Him. Whatever hardship you find yourself facing, surrender to Him. Through such faith, strength, and trust in our Savior, you WILL survive. No matter the waging war upon you, there is power in prayer. He can lift your face and remind you to live.

Face-Lift Action Step #7

ACCORDING TO TIM Keller's book, *Counterfeit Gods*,[18] an idol is "anything more important to you than God, anything that absorbs your heart and imagination more than God, and anything that you seek to give you what only God can give." God provides us clear direction in Exodus 20:3 that we are to have no other gods (idols) before him.

Let's take a look at the idols in our life. Perhaps it's our job (prestige, status, time spent at work). Maybe it's finances (wanting more money, shopping, and all must-haves we long to acquire). It could be relationships (a spouse or loved one, child, or even desire to have the most "friends" or "likes" on social media). And yet, it could even be an action or emotion (pornography, lust, obsession of knowledge, jealousy, malice, worry, or fear). Please note that people and things can be good for us and have their place, but we must be careful to make sure that they never replace our love for the Lord.

Here are some tips on how we can identify, reprioritize, and surrender the idols in our life:

1. What do you spend your time thinking about, dreaming about, or doing? What emotions do you not only feel but cling onto?

_____

_____

_____

_____

_____

_____

_____

_____

_____

2. Have you put any of these ahead of your relationship and time with the Lord?

_____

_____

_____

_____

_____

_____

_____

_____

_____

3. Pray that God will help you be more aware of such idols, and instead refocus your energies on making sure you are not putting anything above or in place of your relationship with Him. After all, He is the only one who can truly meet every need, fulfill our deepest longings, and be not only enough but more than enough.

_____

_____

_____

_____

_____

_____

_____

_____

_____

"Jesus answered, Everyone who drinks this water will be thirsty again, but whoever drinks the water I give them will never thirst. Indeed, the water I give them will become in them a spring of water welling up to eternal life."

JOHN 4:13-14

As we try to reprioritize our life, we can pray, spend time in His Word through daily devotionals, get involved in Bible study, sing praises to Him, join in worship, and take part in fellowship in a church. The answer is not to love our idols less, it is to love, serve, surrender to, and seek God more.

Holly Harding Curby
January 9, 2018

If we are being honest we have all had something in life hit us that has left a scar. Last night I ran out of the house real fast in my pjs and hair tossed up to do a couple of unexpected errands in favor of my daughter. At one errand I ran into a sweet friend who complimented me and I rejectingly shrugged off her compliment. It was what she said next that literally stopped me in my tracks and was one of the most loving things I've ever had said to me, "Ms Holly, why can't you embrace what the rest of us see in you?"

I came home and realized my scars go so deep that when given a compliment such as hers I tend to not be able to accept myself as "enough". I ashamedly went on my knees before God that night and sought His forgiveness for not seeing in me who and how HE created me. It also made me think of how we get our scars to begin with...and from there I thought of two things my dad has often shared: 1) "A faith that cannot be tested cannot be trusted" - Warren Weirsbe. This reminds me that the testing of my faith by Satan is ever so much for my good as it allows me the opportunity to show my faith is real regardless the circumstances, to be authentic in who I claim to be...a princess of the Heavenly King, a believer in Christ who TRUSTS Him through the good and the bad, who walks by faith, not by sight 2) "Blessed is the one who perseveres under trial because, having stood the test, that person will receive the crown of life that the Lord has promised to those who love Him." James 1:12. This reminds me that God still sees us in our times of trial....we are still going to go through the trial one way or another so might as well persevere it, right? Why do I share this? Because my friend, for those of you who have scars, battle wounds, might I remind you that you are NOT alone. That the God of yesterday who kept Noah and his family safe, who parted the sea for Moses, who raised the dead, who turned water into wine, who fed the 5,000 with what should have only fed a little boy, not to overlook the very One who has kept EVERY promise He made...that God of yesterday is STILL the God of today who is still seated on HIS throne and He's got you, His plans can NOT be thwarted (Job 42:2). 6 years ago from this very day I reflected on some very wise words, "In a crises what you chose to do next shows you what you believe about God". So mighty warriors, princess maidens...suit up daily in His armor (Ephesians 6:10-19), rest in Him (Psalm 46:10), know He will fight for you (Exodus 14:14), He created you exactly as He wants you to be (Psalm 139:14), there is a season for every part of our life (Ecclesiastes 3) and trust that He's got you...scars and all (Prov. 3:5-6 and Joel 2:25).

Face-Lift #7

Waging War Is Exhausting—
He Is Our Strength
and Will Never Leave Our Side

"Be strong and courageous.
Do not be afraid or terrified because of them,
for the Lord your God goes with you;
he will never leave you nor forsake you."

DEUTERONOMY 31:6

Chapter 8

Letting Go Brings Healing

OUR FAMILY SEEMED to grow up on hockey. I recall getting to go with my dad to watch the Golden Eagles Salt Lake City hockey team play as a little girl. But it wasn't until our family went through the heartbreak of my sister's devastating canceled wedding back east that hockey seemed to become a part of our entire family. My dad, in an attempt to distract and encourage my sister, began taking her to see the local hockey team play, and before long, it was a path of healing for the whole family. There seemed to be no better family therapy than hearing the swoosh of ice skates attempting to stop abruptly on the ice, crashing sticks colliding, or cheering on the team's favorite player known for getting into a brawl or two each game. So, the night prior to us siblings calling for a serious and dreaded family meeting, it only seemed appropriate to take the family out to a night at a hockey game. The cousins all seemed to have a great time, and my dad appeared so carefree. As much as I tried to enjoy myself, I still had that feeling in my gut that, after this night, everything would change.

My mother, who faithfully weighed in at a local health program each week, exercised daily, ate right, took her vitamins, and had been doing crossword puzzles since I was a kid to keep her mind sharp and alert, had been a little off for a couple of months. At first, I thought it was just her and me having a battle of wills, but then I noticed her misremembering or repeating information she'd already told me, and her typical mannerisms slightly changed. After asking my sister to keep an eye on her during a family birthday party, she also noticed Mom's demeanor was not her typical engaging, joyful self. As a result, we called for a family meeting. As our family gathered in my parents' home that Saturday morning and shared our observations with Mom and Dad, we called our family doctor to have her weigh in on our concerns. We decided as a family that it was better to be safe than sorry, as we were questioning the possibilities of a stroke. So, we took Mom to the emergency room for a checkup. As doctors came and left, tests were taken, and time seemed to have no end. The medical team shared with us that preliminary results appeared to show that Mom had indeed suffered a stroke. My sister and I let out a cheer of relief as we expressed to Mom and Dad that this was relatively good news. The doctors would be able to help Mom avoid future strokes, and there didn't seem to be permanent damage. Just as we were peacefully waiting to be moved to a room for the night while Mom went through some further preventative tests, the doctor hesitantly came back in the room, his face looking troubled. He shared with us that what looked like symptoms of a stroke could actually be a brain tumor. Our hearts sunk in our chests, the breath knocked out of us, and in that moment, our eyes all went to Mom in an attempt to provide solace and strength. We said, "It's going to be okay, Mom. God's got us."

After being admitted to a hospital room, and many more tests throughout the night, we had a false sense of security that the worst-case scenario was the doctors removing the brain tumor. Thinking as such, some of the family took a moment to run home to get their hospital bags, and others went down to the cafeteria to grab a bite to bring back to the room while me and my mom's best friend, Sherrie, stayed in the room to keep Mom company. Guards were down as we enjoyed a good chuckle here and there, until what felt like an overwhelming number of medical staff entered the room. From there, everything became muffled except the words "inoperable brain cancer, glioblastoma." As both Sherrie and I reached out to hold Mom's hand, her eyes didn't appear as shocked by this news as ours did. As the medical team left the room, Mom's favorite Bible verse flooded my mind—

—〰

"I lift up my eyes to the mountains - where does my help come from? My help comes from the Lord, the Maker of heaven and earth"

PSALM 121:1-2

A couple of days later, Mom had brain biopsy surgery—what we now consider one of our biggest regrets. In those waiting days, we sought time together as a family. Everyone slept at the hospital curled up in balls, under chairs, and on the floor, just to be near each other, and to support one another however we could. We played card games, reminisced good times, and tried to encourage Mom prior to the surgery. At the time, we understood this surgery as the next step, a needed procedure to assess how this cancer was behaving and to evaluate how best to treat it, but Mom was not the same afterwards. It left a permanent hair-less scar so prominent on the side of her head, a constant reminder of this battle we were all fighting.

Six days after taking Mom to the hospital, we finally got to take her home. Our next chapter now began as doctor appointments filled the week ahead with a treatment plan for Mom. As a result of the surgery, Mom had difficulty following conversations and struggled to do normal tasks like cooking and writing. We found ourselves wanting to protect Mom and her dignity, and so we tried to kindly ask for friends to hold off on visiting "to best help Mom heal." Healing. What does that even look like when you've just been presented your worst-case scenario in life?

Days after Mom was discharged from the hospital, I had a work meeting at the very hospital where we had just spent the previous week. As I was leaving my meeting, I saw an elderly couple pulling into the parking lot wearing masks over their faces, and I thought, *I wonder what they persevered through this morning just to get here today. What's their story?* It made me think of so many who are going through tough times . . . a loved one passing, a recent diagnosis, illness, a betrayal, financial burdens, loneliness . . . the list goes on and on. I felt such a deep longing to help those I know of going through trials, and I found myself falling short from what I could do to relieve them of their pain and suffering. Then, as if God Himself were trying to get my attention, I thought, *Only Jesus can save!* As much as I want to help the hurting and heal their wounds, I can't, but He can.

- Only Jesus can be with us in our darkest hour (Deuteronomy 31:6).

- Only Jesus can take what Satan has meant for harm and use it for our good (Genesis 50:20).

- Only Jesus can provide for exactly what we need (Philippians 4:19).

- Only Jesus can heal (Jeremiah 30:17).

- Only Jesus can take our ashes and make them beautiful (Isaiah 61:3).

- Only Jesus can save (Ephesians 2:8).

Perhaps you know of friends and loved ones going through tough times, and you long to take away their suffering. Friend, although we can't save them, there is still much we can do. We can pray for them and point them to the One who has great things in store for them (Jeremiah 29:11). The one whose plans cannot be thwarted (Job 42:2). We might not understand His plan (Proverbs 3:5-6;), but I promise we can trust His loving heart (Psalm 9:10). As I watched that couple get out of their car and stagger across the parking lot, I claimed then and there what I would choose to do in the days ahead as we faced this new season with my mom—trust my Savior.

Trust. An action that can be challenging to do if we have limited understanding of who God is. We tend to lean to our own understanding instead of believing that, despite the trial or circumstance, God is good and His ways our higher than ours (Isaiah 55:8-9). When our trust lacks, it's more important than ever to live by faith, not by sight (2 Corinthians 5:7).

It was days later that our family had a meeting with the neuro-oncologist, revealing the results of the biopsy. As we sat at the long table in a large conference room, our family on one side and the doctor across from us on the other, he shared with us news that would forever change our lives. Mom was diagnosed with a grade 4 (of a 1-4 scale, 4 being the worst) brain tumor. Although the plan was to begin chemotherapy and radiation, he answered the unasked question we were all thinking. Mom had no more than one year to live. As tears flowed down my face and my siblings asked many questions, once again Mom didn't seem phased by the news. My dad asked my mom how she felt, and she replied, "It's about how I had anticipated this would go. I knew this wasn't going to have an ending like the others [trials] have. I knew this would be different." We walked out of the hospital that day depleted, scared, and heartbroken, but we also walked out of the hospital side by side as a family, trusting that God was too good to leave us now.

Think about that for a moment. If you were just given less than a year to live, what would be your goals, your desires? How would you live intentionally within your days given? How would you hope people would remember you? Now think about this very day. What is stopping you from living that life? What are you doing now that will be reflective of the legacy you want to leave? And what do you need to start doing to do so?

For us, in the weeks ahead, we truly made our family the priority—we were inseparable. We tried to focus on joy, life, and trust in God's goodness. We gathered at my parents' house nightly for dinner. We'd provide entertainment to Mom and Dad by playing games of speed basketball for them to watch. My sister and I took Mom for what would be her last trip to a beauty salon. And my brother and his wife tried to encourage my daughter (who was extremely close to, and a miniature version of my mom) and provide a temporary distraction for her during this challenging time by taking my daughter on her dream vacation to New York City to see her favorite artist, Toby Mac. We all just tried to keep going.

Emotions swept over us at various times as the weight of Mom's diagnosis set in, yet we were all trying to put on a brave face. We felt so overwhelmed with trying to work, be there for our children, and be solid for my parents, but our lives felt as if they were unraveling.

One night, I vividly recall pulling a book off a shelf to look something up when—CRASH!— my son's special ceramic soccer ball piggy bank my mom had given him fell to the floor. I immediately felt that knot in my gut as I looked at the shattered pieces on the floor. I was quick to turn to apologize to my son when I noticed he was at the kitchen table behind me with his head buried in his hands. He took a deep breath, then turned to me with a gentle smile, got up, kneeled to help me pick up the pieces, and ever so graciously and tenderly said, "It's okay, Mom, accidents happen." In this sweet moment, his gracious response reminded me how, sometimes, when we just want to scream and shout or simply cry, the response someone else needs from us is a patient smile, a gentle word, an understanding tone, or even for us to get down with them and help them pick up the pieces.

So often, these moments in life that lead to intense emotions tempt us to turn to social media (or even phone calls, texts, or emails) and express our feelings, but a wise tip I learned through a leadership training years ago cautioned me on sending, posting, or calling when emotional, tired, or hungry. I don't know about you, but after some of the posts I have read on social media, I think that advice could go a long way with many users.

As our family grieved the continuous decline of my mother and her abilities, I wanted time to stand still—to capture the fullness of each and every day. My social media became my scrapbook. Simply a place to hold moments, a place I could look back and relive the joy and blessings of time with my loved ones, with my mom. Although I felt disengaged from people around me as I sought to intentionally savor these days with my mom, my use of social media served as a window to our reality while also reminding my friends to live in the present in their own lives, as we surely are not guaranteed tomorrow. These social media posts revealed our intentionality in trying to provide something for her to look forward to each day: a picnic in the park, taking the cousins to play as she sat and watched them (a favorite pastime of hers), visits to a local farm to sit and feed the ducks, and wheelchair walks around historic sites. The more treatment she had, the more we noticed her capabilities diminishing and the challenges of our outings increasing. We were grateful for places with golf carts to enjoy the gardens or a train with a wheelchair lift so we could visit the zoo. Our world was opening to the limitations of disabilities, and our hearts had an opportunity to learn deeper compassion for those who face such challenges each and every day. More and more, we found ourselves noticing moments where Mom would have been but couldn't due to her cancer—the emergency room when one of my children got very ill, the baseball games to celebrate a birthday, an evening gala raising funds to fight cancer, and even an awards night for my brother and daughter who raised money for the very hospital treating my mom.

Through it all, we saw God at work again and again. One afternoon, as Mom and I were leaving the hospital after one of her treatments, I was standing beside her in her wheelchair with my hand on her shoulder, gazing at the view while we waited for our valet to arrive. A breeze softly brushed against my face, and I felt as if God was taking a candid picture of the moment of me and my mom together. Out of the blue, I heard a deep voice pass in front of us that expressed some gracious words of encouragement to my mom. He was kind and respectful . . . his words tender and caring. Our car arrived, and with a sturdy arm extended, he offered his assistance to us. Both Mom and I were at complete comfort with this gentleman. As I got in the car, I looked at Mom and asked, "Do you ever wonder if you were just in the presence of an angel?" She smiled and nodded. On the drive home, I thought about how this man, although a stranger, showed such perfect kindness to us through his mere presence, which resulted in us feeling as if we had just felt the love of God touch upon us. Oh, how the saying goes, that one person can make a difference and, as Mahatma Gandhi was credited for challenging us, "Be the change you wish to see in the world."[19] From that day on, I knew I wanted my kindness to especially show to my mom and dad through this challenging time, and so began my commitment to not only attend every doctor appointment with my parents but to begin taking a day off each week to care for my mom morning to night so my dad, Mom's main caregiver, could have a bit of reprieve.

So often in our times of trials, we are tempted to hunker down and spiral into a self-pity party. Years ago, I read somewhere about exchanging self-pity for a servant heart. That when we are down and discouraged, look outward for people to serve and love, and by doing so, we will find that our present state of mind is uplifted and encouraged. I have a little verse in my room that reads,

"A generous person will prosper; whoever refreshes others will be refreshed."

PROVERBS 11:25

This makes me think of that zebra story my mom shared with me.

Let's face it, life can be tough, and we need each other. I think one way we can accomplish this is through encouragement. I've always liked what Barnabas in the Bible is known for. Acts 4:36 shares with us how Barnabas actually had a different name, Joseph, but then the disciples named him Barnabas, as that actually means "son of encouragement." Barnabas was all about focusing on others instead of himself, and he was known as an encourager. Our world, however, tends to be so *me* focused. Social media is flooded with photos of what happiness should look like or seems to indicate that life is all about how many hits, followers, reaches, and downloads you can get—as if that will determine your success, worth, value, happiness, or fulfillment. But just as in the story of the zebra, it's so important to come together and focus on being there for one another, to have each other's backs, and to encourage those around us. When we humble ourselves, put others first, and serve one another, we are able to really see what matters—that life isn't just about *me*.

One of my mom's favorite authors, Patsy Clairmont from Women of Faith Ministries, wrote in her book, "Normal is just a setting on your dryer" about something called Boomerang Joy.[20] She explained that a boomerang has to be flung out with force if it is going to sail through the air and return to the sender. As we learned in chapter 6 regarding encouragement, we too must be intentional in being sensitively bold at looking beyond ourselves to help others. We must be committed that such encouragement is not just a one-time act but may be an ongoing process through act, prayer, time, and words. It must be genuine, not belittle, judge, or base off of merit—a heartfelt encouragement for the purpose of lifting one another up and refreshing them as you may. It may take creativity, as needs vary and talents differ. We must look to the more seasoned and the youthful, as encouragement is not age-biased. We must put the focus on serving others above ourselves, remembering that our cups are filled by serving others. We must accept those who wish to encourage, serve, and love us—and count it all but "boomerang joy."

After six and a half weeks and thirty-three radiation treatments, Mom had bravely and courageously completed the plan for attacking the tumors. In the final two weeks of radiation, our family each exhibited some boomerang joy as we took a day, like we did through Dad's bone marrow transplant, to encourage Mom in some personal way: a colored drawing from her youngest grandson, personalized audio messages from nearly one hundred friends and family throughout the years from me, a song written by her granddaughter, a homemade quilt from her daughter-in-law, a favorite family photo printed on a pillowcase from my sister so that my mom would feel she was being held by us all as she slept, and many other special gifts. We did our best to remind her how strong she was, how loved she is, and that through the strength of Christ, she could keep going (Philippians 4:13).

Something God used to encourage Mom to keep going was a trip through work I earned a little over a year and a half prior to Mom's diagnosis. Although the original plan was to go on my dream vacation to the Mediterranean on a Disney Cruise, a change of finances made us choose plan B, which was Disney World. My parents asked if they could come with us. Little did we know that our plan B would actually be, once again, God's plan A. Ever since Mom's diagnosis, she said that this Disney trip was what she was looking forward to at the end of this first round of radiation and chemotherapy. So, with God's perfect timing of her taking it easy for two weeks post-radiation, and with another two weeks before her next chemotherapy round, we headed off to Disney World for a week getaway. The trip couldn't have gone more perfectly. Mom's favorite animal is a giraffe, so we arranged to stay at a resort that had giraffes. Added to that, I had requested our rooms be located where we could see giraffes from our balconies. Boy, did God deliver. My parents' room overlooked the exact spot where giraffes came to eat every morning. My parents grew fond of one particular giraffe as he happened to be out every morning while they enjoyed breakfast on their balcony. They fondly named him George the Giraffe. There are so many moments I treasure from this trip. My dad appeared so carefree and enjoyed playing around with my kids. My mom seemed to be at such peace as she took in every moment at each park. I often thought of John 15:11 as I watched my parents' faces each day.

"I have told you this so that my joy may be in you
and that your joy may be complete."

My children showed such tender and caring moments as they watched out for my mom and enjoyed goofing around with my dad. Even moments getting caught in a sudden downpour during our poolside dinner seemed to only add to the adventure we were having together. I realized almost every moment of every day how God had provided for this trip, and I was reminded how important it is to

"give thanks in all circumstances, for this is God's will
for you in Christ Jesus."

1 THESSALONIANS 5:18

As our week away came to an end, and reality of flying home set in, we chose to focus on being grateful for the timing of this trip, the memories made together, and to simply say thank you to God for truly "every good and perfect gift is from above" (James 1:17a).

The month after returning from our big trip, I was invited back to the corporate offices of my work. I was so torn and worried that something would happen to Mom, and I wouldn't make it back in time to be with her before she passed. And yet, at the same time, this invitation was a rare invite. After much prayer, I decided to go. I'll never forget talking with my mom and giving her a huge hug before I left. I felt that things wouldn't be the same when I returned, yet I also felt prompted to continue with my trip. On this trip, I was blessed to have a little reprieve in the midst of such a weighing time at home. From fellowship with my Chick-fil-A alumni to getting to tour the Coca-Cola Factory and the Chick-fil-A Football Hall of Fame, even getting to hear Lou Giglio speak and be able to worship with his praise team, it truly was a renewing weekend. The night prior to coming home, I was Facetiming with my mom, and it was the best I had heard her talk in months. Our conversation was full of laughter and smiles, a connection we hadn't had in a while. I went to bed that night deeply grateful for that phone call, longing to see my mom the next day, but I had that feeling that the other "shoe" was about to drop.

As I boarded the plane to come home, I sat in my seat, releasing a peaceful sigh, a reflection of the time I had just experienced while away. Then, just as if I had been punched in the gut, an instinct kicked in to look at my phone before takeoff, and there I saw the other "shoe" dropping. My sister had texted that my mother was having seizures, and they'd probably be taking her to the hospital. I buried my head in my hands and begged God to get me home in time to be with my mom.

That was the longest plane ride home, but God was so faithful and good. I got to the hospital just moments after my mom had arrived there, and I was able to be with her and my family. Hours later, Mom was discharged, and we all knew we had entered a step closer to Mom going home to be with the Lord. It was in that moment that I felt God speaking John 14:27 to me.

"Peace I leave with you; my peace I give to you. I do not give to you as the world gives. Do not let your hearts be troubled and do not be afraid."

God answered my prayers that day. He answered many others in the days to come. Mom had wanted to make it to her seventy-second birthday, and she did. I wanted Mom to make it to my master's degree commencement ceremony, and she did. My dad had hoped she'd make it to their fifty-first anniversary, and she did. We even got to attend the sixtieth anniversary of the church that brought us out to Utah thirty-five years ago, and Dad was the guest preacher. We found it interesting that the very last thing my dad had done before resigning from pastor of that church decades ago was to have a ramp built outside the worship center for disability access. That very ramp was what allowed our family to be able to get up to the worship service for this special day. God is so good. He knows. He provides. As we sang the hymn by Eliza Hewitt, "When we all get to heaven, what a day of rejoicing that will be,"[21] we knew that would be the last church service my mom would attend, most likely the last one we'd attend as a family, and the next time we sang in worship together would literally be when we all get to heaven.

In the following weeks, as the seasons were changing, we decided to venture up to our family cabin for a time of worship. It was a beautiful day with the sun upon our faces, the trees in full color change, and our cherished time together. We had just returned home when I received a call from my dad—my mom was very discouraged. Grateful to only live four houses away, I rushed down to find her and my dad embracing in the living room. She looked up and cried, "I just want to go home." The days that followed, we all wanted to hold on tightly. Every moment, I cherished going down to her house and brushing her hair. Every evening, I cherished singing to her as I tucked her in bed. We had watched my dad tend so lovingly to her every need for over seven months now, lifting her well over forty times a day during wheelchair transports, and growing tired from sleepless nights as she needed care at any given hour. We watched my mom fight through chemotherapy and radiation treatments, going from healthy and independent to needing a cane, then a walker, then a wheelchair just to get around. From the ability to speak to inability to communicate at all. From being completely self-sufficient to being one-hundred-percent dependent on others. Our prayers went from *heal her* to *Lord, please deliver her from this pain.*

It had been a rough day. My dad had worship songs on in the background when he came into their room, where Mom and I lay. He came to her bedside and told her how much he loved her. Surprisingly, she was able to lift her arm, and she initiated a hug with him. He then looked at her and said, "Jan, it's okay to go home." She looked at me with exhaustion, and I reassured her, as Dad did, "Yes, Mom, it's okay to let go and go home. We are here. We love you. We are proud of you. You have fought so hard." We all hugged and wept.

Our family gathered that night for a family sleepover under one roof. As the grandchildren and I gathered—what had become a family moment that brought a smile to Mom's face—we began to sing a song Mom had written while teaching elementary:

"Goodnight now, goodnight now, the clock says we're done. We'll see you tomorrow. Sleep tight, everyone."

As we got to the part of "we'll see you tomorrow," I stopped.... I couldn't sing what I knew in my heart would not be true. We all told her goodnight and gave her a big hug. Then after the kids departed from the room, I looked into my mom's eyes and sang to her the Colin Raye song, "Love, Me"[22] that comforted me after my grandma had passed years ago. It shares of one going ahead of the other, but that other person telling the one that they'll catch up once the stuff they need to get done is finished. Reminding that one that, until that time comes, they will love them, and know that the one loves them too. I kissed Mom for the last time, told her I loved her, and thanked her for being my mom . . . and left the room. To the matriarch of our family, our best friend, mightiest prayer warrior, and biggest cheerleader, the time had come where we had to let go. It was about an hour later, as Mom and Dad lay in bed to sleep, that my mom experienced no more pain, no more suffering. She had fought the good fight, and finished the race, and with a smile on her face, she had gone home to be with the Lord.

As painful as it was, the day of Mom's passing had much to give thanks for. We were able to weep by her side before the mortuary came to compassionately remove her body. Our family gathered in the family room in my parents' home, and we had a time of worship. Dad had even prepared a devotional—"Going forward, my focus is on being grateful." Later that day, we went to the funeral home to begin the preparations to honor Mom. The following day, we escaped to the family cabin, where we all would spend our first night there since building it together. Such a labor of love.

As our family grieved, exactly a month after Mom passed, we found ourselves gathered, once again, in my parents' home. In our time of mourning and loss, Dad shared with us the news he had just learned that very day, that his cancer was back. And just as God had shown us throughout these past months with Mom, we knew no matter the road ahead, God's got us.

Face-Lift Action Step #8

WE CAN GRIEVE many things in life: divorce, deaths, illnesses, job losses, relationships, friendships, miscarriages, addictions, seasons of life ending . . . the list goes on and on.

According to *Good Grief*, by Granger E. Westberg,[23] there are five stages of grief:

- Denial: This can't be happening.

- Anger: Why is this happening?

- Bargaining: I am willing to do anything to change what happened.

- Depression: I can't go on after this happened.

- Acceptance: I know what happened and can't change it, but I must go on.

List things, seasons, people, and situations that you have lost (i.e., jobs, relationships, children living at home, people, etc.):

_____

_____

_____

_____

_____

_____

_____

Think through those losses in your life. Did you complete each stage? If not, what step did you get to before your emotions stopped processing to the next step? Perhaps it's time to complete the remaining steps until you have acceptance and peace with that acceptance.

Remember, although often we have the ability to self-process, sometimes we need assistance through talking with a friend, family member, school counselor, pastor, or grief counselor.

A trusted source I'd suggest is Focus on the Family. They offer counseling consultation and referrals. Call **1-855-771-HELP** (4357), email **help@focusonthefamily.com**, or visit **https:// www.focusonthefamily.com/get-help/counseling- services-and-referrals/** to request a conversation with Focus on the Family's counseling department.

Holly Harding Curby
October 19, 2019

Seasons.

Some come and go so quickly, while others linger on a bit. Our family has been in a season now for nearly 8 months, and just as seasons do, ours is about to change. During this season though we have seen countless ways that the Lord has shined through, reminding us of His beauty, revealing to us His goodness, and providing for our needs. Thank you to everyone who has in some way or another been apart of this season. The meals made with love that have reminded us to eat. The yard being tended to, freeing up our time for other priorities. The cards sent showing care, which have been such an encouragement to us all. The flowers delivered which remind us we are thought of and bring a touch of God's beauty inside. The gifts being dropped off that bring smiles to faces. The visits made to express concern and support. And especially the prayers before the throne of God on our family's behalf as we press into our faith and trust in God's timings and plan.

I am grateful for my work which has allowed flexibility for me to be present where needed. I am grateful for our neighbors who have cared for us through this journey. I am grateful for our church families from throughout the years who have shown us we will always be one in the bond of love. I am grateful for my prayer warriors who are entrusted with my heart 24/7. I am grateful for my family who has herded together to selflessly love and care for each other. I am grateful for my parents who exude selflessness, strength of the Lord, and a genuine faith that stands the test of life itself. And I am grateful for my personal relationship with Christ, which reminds me He is sovereign, loving, will provide for all our needs, strengthen us daily, has a far greater plan than my mind can imagine, comforts every heartache, is the peace that passes all understanding...and works ALL things for good. Only He can take what Satan has meant to harm, and use it for His glory.

There is always something to be thankful for, and in this season, I give God glory, praise and honor for great things He has done... and will continue to do amidst the change of seasons.

Face-Lift #8

Letting Go Brings Healing—
He Is Our Peace

"The Lord gives strength to his people;
the Lord blesses his people with peace."

PSALM 29:11

Chapter 9

The Pandemic Was Challenging

I LIKE A good movie, and especially the thrilling, edge of your seat, action-packed movies. I hear a good thunderstorm, and I think it's a perfect time to watch *Twister* or *Jurassic Park*. If I've had a rough day, *Shooter* is my go-to. So, when I heard of the new virus circulating in China, it was only natural to put in *Contagion* followed by *Outbreak*.

In the weeks to come, this idea of movie themes became less fiction and more nonfiction as the COVID-19 virus began to hit closer to home. There wasn't a known cure. The statistics began rolling out, and it was discovered that this virus affected all ages, not just the elderly as originally suspected.

The news became inundated with COVID-19 updates, otherwise known as the coronavirus. Suddenly, this once movie-like virus was now at our front doorsteps as schools began to close, churches were beginning to live-stream their worship services, restaurants could no longer offer dine-in options, and groups could not gather larger than ten people.

I, the Director of Community and Culture at a well-known restaurant chain, was one of the first impacted at my job. My hours were cut as we no longer offered dine-in, and therefore my help during lunch rushes was no longer needed. My partnership role within the community was brought to a halt as schools were closed and businesses were not catering as they began to work from home. My once full-time hours had very quickly and suddenly changed to minimal hours. Fortunately, as a director, my presence was still needed in some leadership meetings, so I chose to give thanks for each hour received.

Three days into the new normal of my kids not going to school and me not going to work, I was awakened with what felt like the movement from strong winds. As I laid there listening to this rumble, it grew louder and louder, and the walls began to shake. Earthquake! Thankfully, both of my babies had snuck into bed with me during the night, so I quickly yet calmly woke my daughter and told her to get under the doorway. I then picked up my son and bolted for the other doorway of my room. It was a 5.7 quake on the Richter scale, and that was followed by over 100 aftershocks in the week ahead. It was then that I thanked God that I was able to be home with my children during this uncertain time and saw my being taken off the work schedule as God's blessing in disguise.

I think we have all been there. Life hits, and we can't see the reasoning for what is taking place. We wonder "why" instead of trusting in our author who has rhyme to every reason. It is in those unknown moments that we must walk with faith, knowing God is good and his ways are perfect. After that earthquake, I realized God had me at home during this time for a reason, and I tried to relax, not fret, and instead give thanks for this unchartered territory in life which allowed for a slower pace of life and much more time with my children—this unknown pandemic. I also realized that my Facebook could still be an avenue to encourage others during their disruptions of life due to the pandemic. Yes, there are many political, religious, and confrontational statements people choose to make while using a social platform, but as mentioned earlier, we can choose to be the change we wish to see, and we can lead by example.

During those first four weeks at home, I made sure we were good stewards of our time—from having a daily homeschool schedule, including lunch and recesses, to cleaning out the garage, prepping the flower beds, gardening for summer, or even taking on a weekly service project. One week, we prepared seventy-five personalized lunches for a local homeless shelter. Another we spent writing words of appreciation on poster boards and hanging them on the neighbor's back fence, a nurse on the frontlines. We even supported a nonprofit's effort to make care packages for nearly 300 nurses and doctors in the area. We felt honored to be able to give back during this time, and it was a vital reminder to me and my children that things could always be worse.

Before long, we found ourselves on a stay-at-home directive by the governor, otherwise known as *quarantined.* My dad, who was in the midst of infusion treatments due to his returned cancer, was informed by his medical team that he needed to stay away from people . . . including our family. What had gone from stopping by to say hi every day after school, weeknight dinners at our home or his, bike rides and basketball games of horse and pig in his front yard turned into no more contact. Grief set in as not only did we still miss my mom, who had only passed five months prior, but now we couldn't even be in the presence of my dad or sit in his home.

Time seemed to be apocalyptic as the new normal began—wear face masks if leaving your home, have grocery stores deliver food to your front doorstep, see empty parks and playgrounds, most businesses no longer accepting cash, and gestures of a handshake or hug are no longer extended. Those who were still employed primarily worked from home. Unemployment was hitting the daunting numbers of 3.8 million per week and growing. Then I received the news that I was basically being put on furlough. At this point, I had drained every penny in my savings, and I even had to dip into the college fund I set up for my children. The president of the United States fortunately had initiated a Care Act for those in similar situations as mine (not receiving hours from work, yet technically still employed all while caring for children who were out of school due to the virus), who would receive two weeks pay, and then initiated an emergency Family Leave Act that would allow them to receive two thirds of their average pay for up to twelve weeks. This was yet another reminder to trust in God's provision and be assured, as Warren Wiersbe has written, "Never doubt in the darkness what God has told you in the light."[24]

As hours grew scarcer and scarcer, I struggled with the lack of involvement I was having in my business. I felt unwanted and unvalued. My self-esteem took a hit. One of my top love languages is words of affirmation, and all I seemed to hear was "we don't need you." I felt discouraged and confused as to my purpose and why I was being left out when I was one of the pioneers of our executive leadership team. Although I looked for opportunities to show appreciation for my team and care for my leaders, I had to intentionally stop and focus on what God had shown me these past seven years—that no matter how overwhelming things seemed, He had me. I just needed to be still and know that He is God (Psalm 46:10a).

During this time of stillness, I felt led to expand my social media reach by creating a blog (something I NEVER wanted to do). My intent was to include some of my posts that friends and family found encouraging, but I also wanted to provide book reviews to help others in their personal and professional growth and development. I was surprised at how quickly the blog was embraced and the positive feedback I received. Over a year into the pandemic, things still not back to normal, God somehow continued to lift my face, encourage me, and remind me He had purpose for this season. I realized the influence social media was having on people even more—their fears, anger, and anxieties. As many seek to use social media to vent, share life, or reach out, it can often become a sea of distraction, frustration, and deception. My dad has shared the wisdom he heard in a sermon once by Pastor Greg Pouncey—"If you look around, you'll be in distress. If you look within, you'll be depressed. If you look to God, you'll be at rest."[25] Surely, in a season of unknown with the pandemic, our world was needing someone to bring peace, comfort, healing, and a lifting of their face to see the Son.

For years, my mom told me how often people commented about my Facebook postings. Many said they found them encouraging, inspirational, and like a breath of fresh air. My mother often encouraged me to write a devotional book based on such posts. When she was diagnosed with her brain cancer, glioblastoma, that was one of the first things I did. I printed off my social media posts and put them in big binders. That didn't seem to be enough for Mom because she had much more faith in me than I ever have had in myself. It wasn't until this time off that I began to wonder if it was the time to write that book—something I had promised my mom the day she died. As I've shared before, Mom and I used to attend National Women of Faith conferences. One of the main speakers at those conferences, Luci Swindoll, used to say, "Decide to accept the path God has given you (with strength and courage). Don't deny reality, but choose to think on what is praiseworthy of God."[26] That was it! Accepting what is and using this time of God's leadership, I dabbled in writing at the beginning of the pandemic, and before long, I found myself at our family cabin, typing out chapter after chapter. Just as

Mom had encouraged all those years to "look at where God is at in our days," and dad had encouraged, "God isn't the author of confusion but of clarity," I finally saw a new opportunity in what I had once viewed as a disruption (i.e., the pandemic). God was allowing me time to finally bring this book into fruition. He knows each piece of the puzzle, and in His time, if you'll let Him, He'll put it all together in his beautifully designed masterpiece of your life. Pretty much like Jeremiah 29:11 reads,

~

"For I know the plans I have for you," declares the Lord, "plans to prosper you and not to harm you, plans to give you hope and a future."

Yes, there was preparation, there was purpose, and there was peace in the path of a pandemic.

I finished writing my first draft of this book by Mom's birthday, July 26, that same year in 2020. I then proceeded to research publishers, literary agents, and the whole process in preparation of its publishing. Such contacts would result in wise counsel directing me to launch my own coaching and speaking business, create a website, and even start the *Holly's Highlights* podcast.

In 2022, such efforts paid off, and I received the good news from Koehler Books publishing that they wanted to publish my book. And just as if orchestrated by God, there seemed to be purpose in His timings as I signed my book contract at my mom's graveside, with my family gathered around on her birthday—July 26, 2022. And as if to show me that He hears our prayers, catches each tear, and has purpose in our pain, this book is set to release in April 2023—exactly ten years since my divorce, the catalyst for this past decade of events.

A peace ran over me as I thought about Mom's constant

nudging years ago, about all the life experienced these past years, and of what seemed like destruction and distractions in life were leading to God's purpose in and through it. While sitting on that brown leather couch in my former church foyer alongside the Women of Faith representative, I realized why God had called me back in 2009 to the women's ministry. He was using my story to encourage others through Facebook, and preparing a path for what is now *Face-Lift*. Yes, as stated before, there was preparation, there was purpose, and there was peace in the disruptive path of the pandemic.

Face-Lift Action Step #9

ACCORDING TO AN article on Forbes, most people use social media as a hobby, not a job, which is also why they think there is so much scrutiny around the idea that "everyone has experience, few have expertise."[27] Oberlo.com reports the average amount of time spent on social media worldwide is "147 minutes, or two hours and twenty-seven minutes, a day in 2022."[28] An editor I spoke with said her daughter won't even use social media because of the worldly facade presented. So, let's take a personal inventory on our involvement, perspective, and use of social media:

What social media outlets do you have access to?

_____

_____

_____

_____

_____

How do you view social media?

_____

_____

_____

_____

_____

How do you use your time on those social media platforms?

_____

_____

_____

_____

_____

What is the content of your posts (encouraging, attacking, life happenings, political, argumentative, religious, searching for friends, venting, business, etc.)?

_____

_____

_____

_____

_____

What do your posts say about you as a person (values, priorities, beliefs)?

_____

_____

_____

_____

_____

What boundaries might you need to put in place when using social media (time limits, access shared with your spouse to avoid temptations or inappropriate behavior while online, think before you speak, not post when angry, hungry, tired, or emotional)?

_____

_____

_____

_____

_____

What change would you like to see in your social media usage?

_____

_____

_____

_____

_____

How can you start today to be the change you wish to see in social media?

_____

_____

_____

_____

_____

In her book, *Calm, Cool, and Collected*, Arlene Pellicane encourages an acronym of *HABIT* to improve the quality of our relationships, waste less time, and be more productive when it comes to social media:

H—hold down the off button.
A—always put people first.
B—brush daily (live with a clean conscience).
I—I will go online with purpose.
T—take a hike (go outside).[29]

According to a 2021 study published on insider.com,[30] it takes between 18-254 days for a person to form a new habit. Well, as the saying goes, "How do you eat an elephant? One bite at a time." Start today to be that change you wish to see in social media, and then just take it one day at a time.

Holly Harding Curby
March 20, 2020

No Him? No Peace. Know Him? Know Peace.

I am grateful for my personal relationship with Christ and that I have complete peace as we find new normals. I give thanks to God for time at home so I can help my babies with their homework and help be a sense of security. I give thanks my babies are home from school as we value our quality time together and have had some great depths of conversations and priceless teaching moments. I give thanks for quality time together to deepen our relationship and enjoy moments of the day we otherwise would have missed. I CHOOSE to give thanks. Thank you to all those teachers out there putting together lesson plans to help our kiddos still learn and grow. Thank you first responders for always running in, when most are running out. Thank you nurses and doctors for being on the frontline of the unknown. Thank you prayer warriors who go before the throne of God on behalf of so many you don't even know. Thank you, Lord, for the peace amidst the uncertainty of this world, the trust we can have in your Sovereign hand, and the wake up calls to remind us what's the most important thing about life...a personal relationship with you.

It's a good day for a good day. God's got us...NONE of this is a surprise to Him.

Oh...and all those home school parents/teachers out there... RESPECT.

Face-Lift #9

The Pandemic Was Challenging—
He Has a Purpose

"And who knows but that you have come to
your royal position for such a time as this?"

ESTHER 4:14B

Chapter 10

Blessings Are a Gift

WE WERE DAY two of the fifth week into quarantine when it was announced by Utah Governor, Gary Herbert, that schools would not be in session for the rest of the school year. Although we all saw it coming, upon officially hearing the news, my eyes filled with tears. As much as I tried to resist them from flowing, trying to be nonchalant in front of my kids, the tears flowed down my cheeks. I was grateful for this time with my children—it wasn't that. It was the realization that I was significantly decreased in pay for over a month already, and it looked like the next four months would remain the same. Honestly, finances were finally starting to scare me. I had taken quite a bit of time off to help care for Mom, then made it a priority to go with Dad to his appointments when his cancer returned, and now a pandemic. I quickly wiped my tears and turned to God to ask Him to provide as He saw fit and that this would, once again, be an opportunity for me to fully trust in Him, press into Him, and walk by faith in Him.

That very night, after dinner, my children and I went on a walk around the neighborhood. My daughter was telling me some of her future career interests and voiced a concern that she doesn't know quite yet what career she should focus on. I assured her that if she asks God for His direction and guidance, then listen to where He leads, He'll see her through when the time comes. She was only twelve, after all. I began to share with her how I wanted to be a schoolteacher when I was younger. Evidence of such can be seen in photos when I was three years old, sitting on a blanket with my stuffed animals gathered around as I taught them this or that. My bedroom during my early elementary school years had a chalkboard in it and I would line up my stuffed animals and dolls to teach them the Bible. During my latter elementary school years and into middle school, my mom had even put together a school classroom in our basement, including a teacher's desk, a chalkboard, and student desks. I would invite my friends over and teach them our homework. Thanks to a local news television channel's kid's club program, I even ordered us cool student ID cards so we felt official.

After high school graduation, I pursued my generals at a local community college. One of my classes was in public relations. It was love at first class. I quickly changed my focus to graduating with an associate of science in public relations. Still desiring to be a schoolteacher, I attended orientation at the University of Utah. I left feeling discouraged and depleted as I had a gut instinct that I was not to follow that path. Not knowing what I was to study instead of education, I took a year hiatus to achieve my travel and tourism certificate. My brother had told me his company would hire me for their travel needs upon graduation, so I figured this was my new path. Upon graduation, the devastating impact of 9/11 had taken place, which completely changed the travel industry, no longer making it feasible to pursue that as a career.

I was working for a local shopping mall as the customer service supervisor. I was enjoying my involvement in the marketing side of things and offered to help my boss with in-mall events, media relations, and store communications as often as she needed me. Through this, I learned of a communications degree at the university. Researching more, I decided to major in mass communications, unsure of which direction I wanted to go with it but knowing it covered broadcasting, journalism, public relations, advertising, and marketing. Before long, I was promoted to a newly created position of assistant marketing manager for the regional shopping center and, a couple of years after graduating, received a job offer from a local competitor to oversee their redevelopment efforts as the shopping center's marketing director. I accepted the change to prove to myself that I could do the job solo, that is, prior to pursuing what was my dream goal of being a stay-at-home mom. During my time as the marketing director, I had my first child. The mall was amazing, allowing me to bring my daughter to work for a half day each day, even helping create a little nursery in my office.

When the time came to stay home with my daughter, the local chamber of commerce offered me a created position of events director, working from home. Three years later, we welcomed my second child, and the job couldn't have been a better fit to allow us to make ends meet, all while being at home with my babies. Although a layoff was in my future five years later due to budgetary cutbacks, it was only months after the layoff that I overheard a fellow church member talk about an opening position of marketing director at a well-loved national chain's local restaurant, and since I knew the owner through my time working for the regional shopping center, one phone call and a commitment by them to allow some flexibility to be a mom got me the job.

All of this to say, my path would have looked very different as a schoolteacher. God, however, knew what my real path of life would look like. I became a single mom with a personal conviction to never show my children childcare. Do you think I could have stayed home with them after the divorce until they began school if I were a teacher? Do you think I could have had the flexibility I needed through a multi-month hip surgery recovery, staying at the hospital for two weeks during Mom's coma, or the stays during dad's cancer? Would being a schoolteacher have allowed me the flexibility to attend all those court, counseling, and other legal appointments? How about care for my mom the months she was ill? No, God knew exactly what I would need when I would need it. Once again, my plan B was always God's plan A.

As my children and I returned home from that evening walk, I got on my laptop to check my bills, and to my amazement, I had a paycheck's worth of money in my account. As I researched this deposit, I discovered the government had issued checks to aid many of those affected by the pandemic. It was enough to see us through the current month. God is so good.

"Therefore I tell you, do not worry about your life, what you will eat or drink; or about your body, what you will wear. Is not life more than food, and the body more than clothes? Look at the birds of the air; they do not sow or reap or store away in barns, and yet your heavenly Father feeds them. Are you not much more valuable than they?"

MATTHEW 6:25-26

I tell you, my friend, God ALWAYS provides for our needs. I have gone through many battles, absolutely, and just before each battle, God has always been so gracious at providing me with a mountaintop experience to help get me through it. God has always provided hills just before a valley.

- Months after my husband left, our family friends from Missouri invited me and the kids to come visit. I had just enough frequent flyer miles, combined with my son being of free flying age, to make it happen.

- Shortly after that, I was given a free cruise from a major cruise line due to the quantity of cabins I sold on their ships that year, as I was a part-time cruise specialist on the side. This provided a getaway for me, my children, and my mom, just prior to my husband telling me he was divorcing me.

- The next year, shortly after the divorce, our family decided to get away to Durango, Colorado, for a family vacation. Everyone carpooling, sharing meals, and staying at a campground made it affordable to join and all be together, just prior to Mom's poisoning.

- The summer after my mom survived the poisoning, my parents decided to spend any type of inheritance we would receive and take our whole family on a cruise to celebrate life, just prior to Dad's fight against cancer.

- The next summer, they spent the rest of this "inheritance" taking us on another cruise to celebrate my dad's cancer being in remission, just in time for me to then return to face the legal custody battles.

- As the legal battles grew more and more intense, my brother got married, and instead of having a huge wedding locally, he chose to take his wedding budget and fly our family to Hawaii for a small wedding on a beach, just prior to the final part of the legal war.

- We once again found reprieve following that battle on my parent's dream of our whole family going on a Hawaiian cruise that next summer to celebrate my parents' fiftieth wedding anniversary. Hawaii was where they honeymooned and sought R&R during dad's service in the Air Force. We never could have imagined we'd return from that celebration only to soon learn of my mom's diagnosis.

- Even leading up to her death, as I shared earlier, I had earned a trip through my job to Disney World. This trip provided a getaway for me and my kids along with my parents during a crucial time. This would also be the last trip we'd take with my mom before she passed.

I have tried to use my social media page to be authentic about life in hopes of encouraging others, but most importantly to give glory to God through every season of my life. There have been so many seasons experienced. Some seasons came and went so quickly, while others lingered on a bit. As seasons do, they change, reminding us of the beauty within each, revealing to us God's goodness, and always providing for us.

What season of life are you in right now? Is it on the hilltop where life is feeling pretty good? Or is it in the valley where you long for a day of reprieve? These seasons in our lives can help us in so many ways if we look for the lesson to be learned, adopt a growth mindset, and cling to the promises of God as we trust His sovereign hand. Just as we've learned throughout this book, these seasons can:

- Impact our story

- Teach us how to deal with change and trust in God's timings of such change

- Remind us the value of having a supportive group around us to hold us accountable, encourage us, and pray for us through these seasons of life

- Prepare us to do hard things, such as forgive

- Guide us in using our story to help others going through rough times

- Challenge our perspectives and open opportunities to serve others in their seasons

- Relinquish the idols in our life as we grasp the power of prayer

- Bring us to the feet of grief where we can find healing, comfort, and peace as we learn to let go and let God

- And they can shine God's goodness as we see the blessings being refined in the fire

I am grateful for everyone who has in some way or another been a part of my seasons: the meals made with love that reminded me to eat, the yard being tended, freeing up time for other priorities, the cards showing care and encouragement, the flowers showing thoughtfulness and providing a touch of God's beauty inside, the gifts that brought smiles, the visits that expressed concern and support, and especially the prayers before the throne of God on my (and my family's) behalf as we continued to press into our faith and trust in God's timing and plan. I am grateful for my job that allowed flexibility for me to be present where needed. I am grateful to represent a brand with solid integrity, one who took a chance on me, was my means to pursue my master's degree, and showed me once-in-a-lifetime leadership experiences at a very significant point in my life. I am grateful for our neighbors, who have cared for us in some way or another through the journey. I am grateful for our church families, who have shown us we will always be one in the bond of love. I am grateful for my prayer warriors, who are entrusted with my heart twenty-four-seven. I am grateful for my family, who has "herded" together to selflessly love and care for each other. I am grateful for my parents, who have exuded selflessness, strength of the Lord, and a genuine faith that stands the test of life. I am grateful for my personal relationship with Christ, which reminds me that He is sovereign and loving and will provide for all our needs, comfort every heartache, have purpose in our path, and strengthen us daily. He has a far greater plan than my mind can imagine and is the peace that passes all understanding. Only He can take what Satan has meant for harm and use it for His glory. There is always something to be thankful for, and with these seasons, I give God glory, praise, and honor for great things He has done and will continue to do amidst the change of seasons.

The other morning, the seasons were changing. Spring had sprung, and summer was trying to break through. As I was driving to work, I saw an elderly man standing on the sidewalk, eyes closed, and head lifted up, basking in the sun upon his face. Later, as I drove to the Huntsman Cancer Hospital for one of my dad's treatments, a song, "God's Not Done With You," by Tauren Wells began to play on the radio. The repetition of the words "God's not done with you"[31] resonated with me. I'd not heard this before, and as it ended, I was surprised to feel tears stream down my face. The heartache, the battle wounds, even the scars that remain from exhaustion, fears, doubts, and loneliness—they can all be used as part of your story. The point is, as the song boldly declares, "God's not done with you." Oh, how the Lord can use things in our day to speak to us. I thought of those who don't know and don't understand His purpose in their season of life right now. It made me reflect upon that man who, instead of focusing on where he was (standing on a sidewalk with people watching him as they drove by), took the time to enjoy what was happening in the moment (the provision of the warmth upon his face). There is so much to be said about turning our eyes to the Son and basking in the light of His glory and grace, all the while knowing He's not done with us yet.

Oh, precious soul, may we turn our eyes not on our fears, rejections, pains, or injustices, but rather turn our eyes upon Jesus, the One who has chosen you.

"Being confident of this, that he who began a good work in you will carry it on to completion until the day of Jesus Christ"

PHILIPPIANS 1:6

We are not guaranteed tomorrow, so I sure hope that what matters most to me is lived out through my life today:

1. God is my foundation. I am a born-again believer who believes that Jesus died on the cross for my sins. I have confessed that I'm a sinner, asked God to forgive me of my sins, and asked Him into my heart. My desire is to glorify Him in all I do, think about, and say. I want to honor Him in all things, even if and when I'm the only one standing. I am a sinner, yes, but I am saved by grace and am forgiven. My life is His and, although I may not understand life's trials, I trust His sovereign hand. I want to live my life as

the kind of woman that wakes up and puts my feet on the floor, and Satan says, "Oh, crap she's up!" But He sees the presence of God, and runs! Yes, my friend, where God leads me, I will go.

2. My devotion for my children. I have made many sacrifices for them and have truly been at a place where I walked in shoes similar to Abraham, where I had to place them before the Lord and say, "They are yours." I am honored to be their momma, and my daily goal is to show them the love of Christ. I love them to the cross and back. I will do everything possible to show them who Jesus is and lead them to the foot of the cross where, although they have both asked Jesus into their hearts, I hope they choose for themselves to grow, nurture, and walk in that personal relationship with him. From there, I must step back and let God lead them where and how He would choose. I pray over them every night as they sleep, hoping they'll align their hearts with God, praying for who they will marry, and for the character and integrity they will choose to have for themselves.

3. My family is my core. I am proud of the Harding lineage, the dedication of living a life of integrity, being men and women of strong character, and having a strong faith rooted in our Savior. My happy place is anywhere with my family, and my fear is not knowing how to do life without them. We've got each other's backs, hold each other accountable, cheer each other on, and treasure the memories made together. I realize what we have is unique. I do not take it for granted, and I am grateful for it.

Satan's thrown a lot of things at me throughout the years, but I'll still proclaim,

~⊙

"But as for me and my household,
we will serve the Lord."

JOSHUA 24:15B

When we are dealing with difficult situations (which WILL come in life), sometimes God will answer our prayers with a yes, sometimes a no, and often a not yet. One thing I can assure you, though—God has NEVER failed me, and He won't fail you either. As I've shared again and again, there will be times we can't understand His hand, but we can ALWAYS trust His heart. He can use even our darkest days for His glory. Growing pains are hard, but they will be worth it in the end when we see where we've been, how far we've come, and those footsteps where He's carried us through it all. Challenges in life are a walk of faith, for sure. An acronym for FAITH that my dad has always used to help drive this understanding home to us kids was

Forsaking
All
I
Trust
Him

We can choose to ignore challenges (but they are still there), run from them (but they may follow us or at the very least cheat us of much-needed growth), or we can opt to trust God through them.

I once had a conversation with a coworker who stated, "To trust God is to relinquish control of my life—and I can't give up that control." Oh, friend, I can attest that we are far better off allowing God to be in the driver's seat than to try and take the wheel ourselves. So many times, God has stepped in on my behalf and blocked the enemy's arrows, declaring, "Not today, Satan." Surrendering such control is actually what gives me peace in knowing that no matter what comes my way, it truly is well with my soul.

I don't always understand what God is doing in life. Women's speaker Beth Moore said it perfectly in one of her studies, "When we trust our lives to the unseen but ever-present God, He will write our lives into His story and every last one of them will turn out to be a great read. With a grand ending."[32] He is the author of my story. In the end, it will be His masterpiece which hopefully ends with:

"well done, good and faithful servant!"

MATTHEW 25:23A

and

"I have fought the good fight,
I have finished the race,
I have kept the faith"

2 TIMOTHY 4:7

Precious one, fight your good fight. Finish the race God has set for you. And keep that faith. I've often been asked how the Word of God comforts me, strengthens me, and guides me, a golden thread throughout this book. Well, it requires time with the Lord. Meditating on His word day and night. Memorizing the scripture so that you can claim it as you walk through your journey. Talk about it with your children. Put up décor with scripture in your home. Have a verse you focus on learning each week or even month if needed. Highlight and date those verses in your Bible, even mark which verses felt applicable for the season of life you are in. But no matter what you face, remember that you can enjoy that journey when you know who's with you every step of the way, and hiding God's Word in our heart (Psalm 119:11) helps us do just that. Live our life knowing God's got us.

Thank you for allowing me the opportunity to share my story with you. I hope that no matter what challenges of life you've seen, the trials you are currently walking through, or the ones that are up ahead, you'll be reminded our seasons may change, but our Creator does not. Oh, how thankful I am that time and time again God sees us, He knows our needs, He feels our hearts, He hears our cries, and He graciously, lovingly, mercifully, ever so tenderly reaches down and gives us a face-lift.

Face-Lift Action Step #10

DO YOU KNOW Jesus as your personal Lord and Savior? If not, there is no better time than right now. It is not by works, it is not by who you know or your status in your occupation, rather it is simply by having a personal relationship with Jesus. I honestly don't know how people go through hardships, or life, for that matter, without His presence in their life. He never promised us this life would be easy, but He does assure us in Matthew 19:26 that, with Him, all things are possible. Here's how to plainly and simply ask Jesus to come into your heart:

Admit that you are a sinner (have made mistakes that are against the Lord). Ask the Lord to forgive you of those sins.

"For all have sinned and fall short of the glory of God"

ROMANS 3:23

Believe in your heart that God sent His one and only son, Jesus, to die for our sins, and on the third day, He raised him from the dead (he keeps his promises). Therefore, God is the One in whom you want to put your trust.

"God demonstrates his own love for us in this: While we were still sinners, Christ died for us"

ROMANS 5:8

"For God so loved the world that he sent his one and only Son, that whoever believes in him shall not perish but have eternal life"

JOHN 3:16

Confess that Jesus is Lord. It's one thing to believe it in your heart, but another to actually confess it out loud and want to commit to live for Him in your daily life. So, go ahead and tell your friends, your family, whomever you feel should hear the good news.

"If you declare with your mouth, "Jesus is Lord," and believe in your heart that God raised him from the dead, you will be saved"

ROMANS 10:9

I'd invite you to pray the following:

"Dear Lord Jesus, I know that I am a sinner, and I ask for your forgiveness. I believe you died for my sins and rose from the dead. I turn from my sins and invite you to come into my heart and life. I want to trust and follow you as my Lord and Savior."[33]

If you prayed that prayer for the first time, oh how I would love to rejoice and celebrate with you. I'd invite you to let me know by reaching out to me at hello@hollycurby.com. I assure you, that will be the best decision you have ever made.

Perhaps you already have a personal relationship with the Lord. Who do you pray comes to know Him?

_____

_____

_____

_____

_____

Who can you reach out to and extend the love of Christ?

_____

_____

_____

_____

_____

Who may need to read this book as an encouragement that there is hope in the One who can be the lifter of their head, resulting in a total face-lift?

_____

_____

_____

_____

_____

I'd also encourage you to write your own story to share with those you may encourage, inspire, and equip. Check out the *How to Write Your Story (your testimony)* resources found in the back of this book.

Holly Harding Curby
August 11, 2018

Ever have a memory hit you that brought you to your knees? Today we did an unexpected detour and as I was following my parents' car we came around the bend to this golf course where I saw this view which took me back to 5 years ago. I vividly recall bicycling here with my family and feeling the Lord's presence as I saw this very view and thinking, "just think if you were out there amongst all those peaks and jagged rocks and you gave up... when just across the desert there was this lush green grass that awaited you?" It was then I felt as if the Lord was speaking to my soul saying, "this is going to be hard, scary, and even painful, but don't miss the blessings I have for you."

Today as I gazed at this scenery tears began to flow down my cheeks, and in awe at His goodness I thanked God for bringing me through some very difficult years. The kids of course couldn't read my mind nor hear my thoughts, but their hearts compassionately empathized with mine as they both, without a word, unbuckled their seatbelts and from behind me put their hands on my arm and shoulder. Allee then began to sing, "You're God of the hills and valleys, and I am not alone." (Tauren Wells) Peyton and I chimed in and the three of us sang praise unto God as we drove away to catch back up with my parents. Following our song I explained my moment of tears to them simply by saying "God is good, all the time" to which they replied, "and all the time, God is good." Go ahead...open your eyes, quiet your voice, and listen with your soul...where do you see God in your day and what does He have to say? No matter what you've been through, where you are at, or what lies ahead...He's there. Just look....

"I will instruct you and teach you in the way you should go; I will counsel you with my loving eye upon you." Psalm 32:8

Face-Lift #10

Blessings Are a Gift—
Give Thanks to God and Count Your Blessings

"Give praise to the Lord, proclaim His name; make known among the nations what he has done."

—PSALM 105:1

Bonus Chapter

Chapter 11

Living Life Anyway

AS WE FINISH our walk in the garden and prepare to part ways, I want to give you a warm embrace and a final thought to encourage you. As you step back into life and attempt to take what you've connected with here and use it as a resource to help with your own challenges, I hope that one day your mess can become your message. Just as my mother cautioned me, though, you might just have to go through it first.

During such time, you may feel that you've taken a step back, gone off course, or perhaps failed the test of the trial at hand. May you remember that failure is not final, fatal, or forever—and it doesn't define you, it refines you.[34]

At the same time, maybe you filled out all the action steps and have good intentions at following through, but you figure you'll get to implementing them in your life one of these days. Well, as my favorite sermon of my dad's is titled, do you really want to spend "one more night with the frogs"? The lesson comes straight from scripture in Exodus 8:1-15. Pharaoh is enslaving the Israelites when the Lord sends Moses to tell Pharaoh to set his people free. As a result of Pharaoh not listening, the Lord sends a plague of frogs. Pharaoh tells Moses and Aaron that he'll let the people go if the Lord will just take away the frogs. Moses agrees and asks when Pharaoh wants the frogs removed, to which Pharaoh replies, "Tomorrow." Friend, whatever you are going through in life, do you want to spend one more night with the frogs, or would you rather have that "plague" in your life dealt with today?

Sometimes things may get worse before they get better, but if we give it our all, we can trust that He is all we need. There may be risks we have to take, fears we must face, but rarely can we make a lasting impact while also playing it safe and residing in our comfort zone. You may have to take a stand, even when you are the only one standing. May you choose to press through, refuse to sink, and not just survive but thrive anyway—just as Mother Theresa shares in her poem, "Anyway."[35]

> "People are often unreasonable, illogical and self-centered;
> Forgive them anyway.
> If you are kind, people may accuse you of selfish, ulterior motives;
> Be kind anyway.
> If you are successful, you will win some false friends and some true enemies;

Succeed anyway.
If you are honest and frank, people may cheat you;
Be honest and frank anyway.
What you spend years building, someone could
destroy overnight;
Build anyway.
If you find serenity and happiness, they may be
jealous;
Be happy anyway.
The good you do today, people will often forget
tomorrow;
Do good anyway.
Give the world the best you have, and it may never
be enough;
Give the world the best you've got anyway.
You see, in the final analysis, it is between you and
your God;
It was never between you and them anyway."

As I shared before, God can't use an unbowed head, but we can bow it in complete surrender to His will. May we embrace peace, comfort, and hope, knowing that no matter what comes our way He will lift our heads and give us a face-lift.

Acknowledgements

GOD—YOU ARE THE true author of this book as you are the author of my life. I am nothing without you, and everything because I am yours. Thank you for being my firm foundation, the bearer of life, and the sustainer of it. I know, with you, I am never alone. You are my helpmate, my healer, my defender, my protector, and my provider of all. You hold me, comfort me, and—time and time again—lift me up. I surrender all to you, Lord. Thank you for making me a princess because YOU are my king.

Mom and Dad—you are my anchor. My biggest cheerleaders and my core. In a day and age where everything is built to be disposable, your love is one I've been blessed to see lived out, one built on a solid foundation that stands the test of time. You are exemplary. Through your marriage, you have exuded love, faithfulness, and commitment to the sacred vow taken over fifty years ago. You have served others side by side, each other selflessly, and our family sacrificially. Thank you for raising us in the Lord, being present at everything for us kids and the grandkids, and spending quality time with us to connect deeply. Thank you for being vulnerable, real, honest parents of high integrity, with strong morals, values, and beliefs. Mom, you were my best friend. Dad, you are my rock. You both leave quite a legacy. I love you both more than you'll ever know.

Christy and Scott—I am grateful for each of you and the memories we have together. Although both of you are older than me, I feel it my responsibility to protect you. Thank you for your thoughtfulness, your selflessness, for doing this life with me, and for putting our family "herd" as a priority in your life. You are my connection to my past and the ones I want to continue to do life with in the future. You are my home. I love you greatly.

Allee—you are living proof that God knows the desires of our heart, answers prayers, and can strengthen us for anything and everything that comes our way. Your wisdom is well beyond your years. Your courage—inspirational. No words adequately express how proud of you I am and how very much I love you. Thank you for always believing in me and being one of my biggest cheerleaders. You shine brightly, baby girl. May you always shine for Him.

Peyton—you are my boy (to which I love to hear you reply, "You're my girl"). You are my gift from God, and I pray for you to continue to grow in your walk with the Lord to become a man after God's own heart (Acts 13:22). You are brave and energetic, your heart is big, and your smile lights up a room. I thank God for your compassionate heart, your desire to connect, and the bond that we share. I am proud of you! I love you, bubbs.

Tim—for believing in me, pushing me, and encouraging me when I needed it . . . and for your loving faithfulness to my sister.

Dominic, Isaac, Stetson, and Austin—I hope that as you have walked parts of this journey too, you have seen God's goodness, power, faithfulness, and love. He will never fail you! Know you are each in a family who loves you greatly, is always here for you, and believes in you.

Amanda (Mandy)—you were my lifeline at my deepest hour. Your selfless sacrifice of time on a weekly basis was invaluable. Thank you for always pointing me to His Word, holding me accountable, encouraging me to press forward, and for praying so fervently for me and my family.

Allison, Christina, and Dana— you came alongside of me and lifted my arms at a crucial turning point in life.

Holly and *Stephanie*—you stepped in and added prayer support to alleviate the burdens as seasons of trials continued throughout the years.

Becky O., Debbie, and Connie—you were Mom's faithful, fervent prayer warriors throughout my entire life and therefore took on your committed love and dedication of praying for me (and my whole family) through this journey. Thank you all for being my priceless, mighty princess prayer warriors.

Levere—you stepped in and met a basic need once my former husband left (taking out the trash cans to the curb) and mowing my lawn while I was helping to care for my mother. You truly are a neighbor who "takes care of the widows and orphans" (James 1:27). Thank you.

Carrie—thank you for uniquely ministering to me in a way I will never forget . . . a wheelchair ride around the block during my recovery from hip surgery. Those breaths of fresh air were uplifting and encouraging during a restraining time. Your creativity has inspired me in how I seek to meet the needs of others. Thank you!

Jessica, Bev, Holly, Chris, Becky H., Tom, and Shirley—you were my constant prayer warriors in the court room. Thank you for caring, showing up, and bathing us in prayer. I'll never forget the court date where I could feel the wings of angels spread out over me just by your presence there. Your time, ministry through prayer, and care for my family are priceless.

Dan and Sherrie—thank you for loving our family through all of this and being there in so many ways through this journey. You and my parents truly are kindred spirits, and we are blessed to have you as family.

Tammi, Susan, Jay and many others who served, cared for, and prayed for our family through these journeys – I have no words to adequately express our gratitude. Thank you!

To my Chick-fil-A family—for your understanding, flexibility, patience, and support during many of these seasons of life, for providing me my role on the team and allowing me to do what fulfills me - loving on others, showing care for our team, and inspiring people to take good care of each other; it is a privilege, thank you!

To Dan Cathy and my Chick-fil-A Foundation alumni family— you played an instrumental part in the lifting of my head. Thank you for seeing value in me, believing in me, cheering me on, and investing in me. My experiences through the Leadership Fellows program and as a scholarship alumni are ones I truly treasure.

"To GOD be all glory, great things
HE hath done."[36]

—FANNY J. CROSBY

Group Discussion Guide

WHETHER READING *FACE-LIFT* individually or as a group (church group, friends, coworkers), this discussion guide is to help you dive deeper into each chapter for personal reflection, encouraging connection and reminding you that you are not alone.

Chapter 1: In the Beginning—Embracing Our Story

1. Briefly introduce yourself to the group. Share what your biggest takeaway was from your life timeline.

2. Why is it important to look back on our high points and low points in life?

3. How has what you have been through prepared you for where you are?

4. What is your typical response to trials: fight, flight, freeze, or desire to grow?

5. What are your thoughts about social media? Which platforms do you use, and how do you use them?

6. What are you hoping to learn or get out of reading this book?

7. How has this chapter encouraged, inspired, or equipped you?

Chapter 2: Change Is Hard—Seeing God's Timing

1. How do you deal with conflict?

2. What are some of the risks of not facing conflict directly?

3. What are the challenges you face when dealing with change?

4. What have been some of the biggest changes in your life, and how did you deal with them?

5. How can we intentionally look for God's promises and blessings during our challenges and changes in life?

6. What challenges and/or changes are you currently going through, and how do you see God's timing of them in your life?

7. If comfortable, share a time you faced a giant in your life. What was challenging about facing that giant? What resources and/or tools did you use for the battle? What was the end result of conquering your Goliath? Is that giant still something that resurfaces? If so, how are you prepared for follow-up matches with that giant?

8. How has this chapter encouraged, inspired, or equipped you?

Chapter 3: Isolation Isn't Easy—Seeking a Support Group

1. Why do we need a close-knit support group?

2. What are the challenges of having such a group?

3. How do we know who to have in our supportive group to hold us accountable, and how do we gather them around us to do life together?

4. When have you felt a situation in life was too much? How did others help hold you accountable and/or encourage you during that difficult time? How did that impact you during that situation?

5. What precautions should we take using social media when going through seasons of life?

6. How has this chapter encouraged, inspired, or equipped you?

Chapter 4: Heartache Is Painful—Processing Forgiveness

1. What are your initial thoughts, feelings, and/or reactions to forgiveness?

2. What tends to hold us back from forgiving?

3. Is an apology necessary for forgiveness? Explain your answer.

4. How should we deal with reoccurring offenses?

5. Sometimes we want others to sympathize with us when we've been wronged or were accused of wronging someone. How can social media play a role in this?

6. Is there someone you need to forgive? Write a letter forgiving that person, then crumble it up, pray, ask God to free you from that injustice done to you (or the one you're accused of), and throw it away.

7. How has this chapter encouraged, inspired, or equipped you?

Chapter 5: Poisoned Leads to Forgiveness—Sharing Our Story

1. Why is it important to focus on our blessings when going through a trial, instead of focusing on the trial itself?

2. Looking back on your timeline from chapter 1, what is something good that has come from a trial or challenge in your life?

3. How can we persevere through tough times when we are worn, exhausted, and/or feeling alone?

4. Why can revenge be tempting? How can we resist taking justice into our own hands?

5. How have you encouraged, inspired, or equipped others? How have you seen others use their challenges in life to encourage, inspire, or equip others?

6. How has this chapter encouraged, inspired, or equipped you?

Chapter 6: Cancer Is Devastating—Open-Mindedly Serving Others

1. Why are we tempted to wallow in self-pity when facing trials?

2. How can we change our perspectives when going through tough times?

3. Share a time when someone encouraged you in a unique way.

4. What prevents us from serving others when they are in need? And how can we overcome these limitations/excuses to help others experiencing hardships?

5. What has helped you get through other tough times in your life?

6. What are some practical steps we can take in developing a servant-heart?

7. How has this chapter encouraged, inspired, or equipped you?

Chapter 7: Waging War Is Exhausting—Prayerfully Surrendering Our Idols

1. What challenges do you or perhaps others face when it comes to believing in prayer?

2. Why can praying for others be difficult, especially for those who have hurt us?

3. When have you seen prayer be powerful and effective in your life?

4. How can our top priorities, passions, things, or ones we hold dear become idols?

5. How can we prevent such things from becoming idols in our life?

6. How has this chapter encouraged, inspired, or equipped you?

Chapter 8: Letting Go Brings Healing—Coping With Grief

1. Share a time you grieved a loss. What was helpful? What was not helpful? What surprised you about your grief?

2. Can social media play a role in our grieving? Explain.

3. How do you want to be remembered? What legacy do you want to leave?

4. Having a personal mission statement can help us live our life full of purpose. Check out "How to Write a Personal Mission Statement" toward the back of this book. This may help you leave that desired legacy. If you've already completed it, share your statement with the group.

5. How has this chapter encouraged, inspired, or equipped you?

Chapter 9: The Pandemic Was Challenging—Re-evaluating Disruptions and Social Media

1. How do you respond to distractions and disruptions in life?

2. How can disruptions become opportunities or transformative moments in our life?

3. How can we set an example for others in how we handle life's distractions and disruptions? Who are some of those we directly influence or those who may just be watching us?

4. What disruptions are you experiencing in life right now? What are you learning from them? Any blessings in

disguise? Explain.

5. How can disruptions direct us to our destiny or purpose, and how can we find joy in that discovery?

6. How has this chapter encouraged, inspired, or equipped you?

Chapter 10: Blessings Are a Gift—Looking At the Silver Lining

1. What aspects of Holly's story could you most relate to?

2. What did you find surprising about this book?

3. Share a favorite quote from the book. How did this quote resonate with you?

4. What did you learn from, take away from, or get out of this book?

5. Have any of your views or thoughts of social media changed after reading this book?

6. How has this book encouraged, inspired, or equipped you to intentionally live your life full of purpose?

Resources

How to Share Your Story (Testimony)

"But in your hearts revere Christ as Lord. Always be prepared to give an answer to everyone who asks you to give the reason for the hope that you have. But do this with gentleness and respect."

—1 PETER 3:15

SHARING YOUR STORY of how you came to know Jesus as your personal Lord and Savior is one of the greatest ways you can show others God's love. Remember, write out your story just the way you speak, as if speaking to a friend. Your story should be something you can share in a casual conversation with anyone at any time, so try to keep it between three and ten minutes in length. Practice saying your testimony so that you can keep it concise when the time is ready to share it.

Use the following questions to help guide you when writing your story. Basically, share what your life was like before Christ, how you came to know Him, and how your life has changed after coming to know Jesus as your personal Lord and Savior. You can read an example of a testimony in Acts 22:1-21 when Paul shares his story. Before you begin, pray, asking God to guide you and provide both wisdom and discernment as you write. Your testimony will be a powerful tool as you share about God and His goodness to others, so make sure it begins in prayer.

1. BEFORE: What was your life like before coming to know Christ? Where or in what did you find your identity (your value)? What were you doing to feel fulfilled or happy? What made you realize your need for a personal relationship with Jesus?

_____

_____

_____

_____

_____

_____

_____

_____

_____

_____

_____

_____

_____

_____

_____

_____

_____

_____

_____

_____

_____

_____

_____

_____

2. HOW: How did you come to know Jesus as your personal Lord and Savior? What challenges, disbeliefs, or obstacles did you have to face to surrender your life to God? Do you have a favorite Bible verse, and if so, why did it become your favorite?

3. AFTER: What does life look like now that you have Jesus
   in your heart? How is it different than before? How does
   having a personal relationship with Christ impact your
   decisions, how you face challenges, and life overall?

   _____

   _____

   _____

   _____

   _____

   _____

   _____

   _____

   _____

   _____

   _____

   _____

   _____

   _____

   _____

   _____

   _____

   _____

   _____

   _____

(For more space, please refer to the notes section in the back.)

How to Create a
Personal Mission Statement

HAVING A PERSONAL mission statement can help us live our life full of purpose. A personal mission statement helps us clarify our goals, set boundaries, prioritize our values, and live out our "why."

Create your personal mission statement by asking yourself these questions:

1. Write down what matters most to you. What/who do you most value? What are you passionate about in life?

_____

_____

_____

_____

_____

_____

_____

_____

_____

_____

2. What do you enjoy doing? What are you good at? What talents or skills make you unique?

_____

_____

_____

_____

_____

_____

_____

_____

_____

3. What are some goals you have for yourself (both personally and professionally)? What would you like to achieve? What are your priorities?

_____

_____

_____

_____

_____

_____

_____

_____

_____

4. How do you want to be remembered? What impact do you hope you make on others, in your family, at your work, or in the world? What do you want others to say about you? Why do you want to be remembered this way?

_____
_____
_____
_____
_____
_____
_____
_____
_____
_____

Now bring these responses into crafting your personal mission statement. Start with a draft or two, and reword it until you've nailed what motivates you, inspires you, and encourages you to pursue that mission in your life. Your personal mission statement should reflect you and declare your "why."

Consider using action words such as inspire, create, support, make, use, write, be, share, encourage, provide, help, save, bring, become, or build when defining your mission statement's purpose.

TO (action word)   (goal) _____

TO _____

Example: To glorify God in all I say, think, and do.

Now let your light shine, and share who you are with the world. I encourage you to post your mission statement on your social media (if applicable). I would enjoy hearing your personal mission statement too. Please tag me on Facebook **@Hollyshighlights** and on Instagram **@hollycurby**.

Scripture Memory Verses

TO KNOW GOD'S Word in our hearts, as Psalm 119:11 instructs, after finishing each chapter, cut out the related verse. Place the verse wherever it may help you memorize its scripture: on the bathroom mirror, in your Bible, next to your bed, on the fridge, etc.

Additional ways to memorize scripture:

- Place scripture décor throughout your home.

- Write down verses on note cards and keep them with you.

- Write scripture on sticky notes and place them in prominent places around your home and/or office.

- Put scripture in a song.

- Have a verse of the week for your family to learn together.

- Make scripture games (such as a memory game where you match the verse and its reference, or a puzzle where you have to put the pieces together to reveal the verse).

Above all, ask God to help you memorize scripture.

"I have hidden your word in my heart
that I might not sin against you."

—PSALM 119:11

Chapter 1

"For I know the plans I have for you,
declares the Lord.
Plans to prosper you and not to harm you,
plans to give you hope and a future."

—JEREMIAH 29:11

- ✂ - - - - -

Chapter 2

"Trust in the Lord with all your heart and lean
not on your own understanding;
in all your ways submit to him, and he will
make your paths straight."

—PROVERBS 3:5-6

Chapter 3

"Not giving up meeting together, as some are in the habit of doing, but encouraging one another – and all the more as you see the Day approaching."

—HEBREWS 10:25

- ✂ - - - - -

Chapter 4

"See, I am doing a new thing! Now it springs up; do you not perceive it?
I am making a way in the wilderness and streams in the wasteland."

—ISAIAH 43:19

Chapter 5

"I lift up my eyes up to the mountains –
where does my help comes from?
My help comes from the Lord, the Maker of
heaven and earth."

—PSALM 121:1-2

Chapter 6

"You intended to harm me,
but God intended it for good to accomplish
what is now being done,
the saving of many lives."

—GENESIS 50:20

Chapter 7

"Be strong and courageous. Do not be afraid or terrified because of them, for the Lord your God goes with you; he will never leave you nor forsake you."

—DEUTERONOMY 31:6

- ✄ - - - - -

Chapter 8

"The Lord gives strength to his people; the Lord blesses his people with peace."

—PSALM 29:11

Chapter 9

"And who knows but that you have come to your royal position for such a time as this?"

—ESTHER 4:14B

- ✂ - - - - - -

Chapter 10

"Give praise to the Lord, proclaim His name; make known among the nations what he has done."

—PSALM 105:1

RESOURCE RECOMMENDATIONS

Books

The Love Dare by A. Kendrick and S. Kendrick

Forgiving What You Can't Forget by Lysa Terkeurst

Good Grief by Granger Westberg

10 Seconds of Insane Courage by Garrett Gravesen

Goliath Must Fall by Louie Giglio

Online

Divorce Care
   https://www.divorcecare.org

Focus on the Family Counseling
   https://www.focusonthefamily.com/get-help/
   counselingservices-and-referrals/

Now Discover Your Strengths Personality Test
   https://www.gallup.com/cliftonstrengths/en/286556/
   ndys.aspx

The 5 Love Languages Quiz
   https://5lovelanguages.com/quizzes/love-language

Experiences

Marriages: Weekend to Remember
   https://www.familylife.com/weekend-to-remember

Families: Glorieta Family Camp
   https://glorieta.org/camps/family-camp/

Movies

Fire Proof

Redeeming Love

War Room

Bible Studies

The Armor of God by Priscilla Shirer

Esther by Beth Moore

HomeBuilders Couples Series

Endnotes

Chapter 1

1   Wiersbe, W. (2008). *Be Resolute (Daniel): Determining to Go God's Direction* (2nd Ed.). Colorado Springs, CO: David C. Cook.

2   Brock, M. (2020) *She Speaks* Women's Conference. Charlotte, NC. August 1, 2020.

Chapter 2

3   Giglio, L. (2017) *Goliath Must Fall*. Nashville, TN: Thomas Nelson.

Chapter 3

4   In *Webster's Revised Unabridged Dictionary* (1913). Springfield, MA: C&G Merriam Co.

5   Author unknown, "*Thanksgiving Observance*," Country Living, December 6, 2022, https://www.countryliviging.com/life/inspirational-stories/g33540159/thanksgiving-poems/

6   Story, L. (2011). Blessings. On *Blessings* (CD). Brentwood, TN: INO Records.

Chapter 4

7   Gaither, B., Gaither, G. (2001). Because He Lives. On *A Billy Graham Music Homecoming Volume 2*(CD). Santa Monica, CA: Universal Music Distribution.

8   Graalman, M., Hammitt, M., Prevost, P., Rohman, C. (2012). Promises. On *Run* (Digital). Brentwood TN; Sparrow.

9   Kendrick, A., Kendrick, S. (2008). *The Love Dare* (1st Ed.). Nashville, TN: B&H Books.

10   Terkeurst, L. (2020). *Forgiving What You Can't Forget*. Nashville, TN: Nelson Books.

Chapter 5

11   Mullins, R. (1991). Sometimes By Step. On *The World as Best as I Remember It, Vol. 1* (CD). Franklin, TN: Reunion Records.

12   Stevens, C., Barlowe C. (2014). Fighter. On *Ready to Fly* (CD). Franklin, TN: Gotee.

13   Powers, M. (1964). *Footprints in the Sand.*

14   Heath, B., TobyMac; Stevens, C. (2012). Steal My Show. On *Eye On It* (CD). Brentwood, TN: Forefront Records.

Chapter 6

15   *What Cancer Cannot Do* (n.d.). Retrieved from https://www.marywashingtonhealthcare.com/Posts/2016/August/What-Cancer-Cannot-Do.aspx.

Chapter 7

16   Capehart, C., Tunie, C., Winans, C. (2008). Waging War. On *Thy Kingdom Come* (CD). Brentwood, TN: Puresprings Gospel.

17   Moore, B. (2010). *David, Seeking a Heart Like His.* Nashville, TN: LifeWay Christian Resources.

18   Keller, T. (2011). *Counterfeit Gods.* New York, NY: Penguin Books.

Chapter 8

19   Morton, B. (2011). *Falser Words Were Never Spoken.* https://www.nytimes.com/2011/08/30/opinion/falser-words-were-never-spoken.html.

20   Clairmont, P. (1998) *Normal is Just a Setting on Your Dryer.* Colorado Springs, CO: Focus on the Family.

21   Hewitt, E. (1898). When We All Get To Heaven. In the *African American Heritage Hymnal.* Winona, MN:GIA Publications, Inc.

22   Ewing, S., Barnes, M. (1991). Love, Me. On *All I Can Be* (CD). Los Angeles, CA: Epic.

23   Westberg, G. (2020). *Good Grief.* Minneapolis, MN: Fortress Press

Chapter 9

24   Wiersbe, W. (2006). *The Bumps Are What You Climb on: Encouragement for Difficult Days*. Ada, MI: Fleming H. Revell Company.

25   Boom, C. (1971). *The Hiding Place*. Houston, TX: World Wide Publications.

26   Swindoll, L. Women of Faith Conference.

27   Zfat, N. (2017). *An Open Letter to People Who Don't Use Social Media*. Forbes. December 6, 2022. https://www.forbes.com/sites/nataliezfat/2017/04/17/an-open-letter-to-people-who-dont-use-social-media/?sh=21a83ac352f4

28   Oberlo. December 6, 2022. https://www.oberlo.com/statistics/how-much-time-does-the-average-person-spend-on-social-media

29   Pellicane, A. (2020). *Screen Kids*. Chicago, IL: Northfield.

30   Manoylov, MK. (2022). *How long does it take to break a habit? 5 science-backed tips to change unhealthy habits*. Insider.com. https://www.insider.com/guides/health/mental-health/how-long-does-it-take-to-break-a-habit

Chapter 10

31   Wells, T., Herms, B., Weisband, E. (2017). Hills and Valleys. On *Hills and Valleys (CD)*. Franklin, TN: Providence Music Group.

32   Moore, B. (2008). *Esther*. Nashville, TN: LifeWay Press.

33   *Sinner's prayer*. Wikipedia. December 6, 2022. https://www.google.com/search?client=safari&rls=en&q=the+sinner%27s+prayer&spell=1&sa=X&ved=2ahUKEwiC4P7Erun7AhWYj4kEHR5_Ac4QBSgAegQIBxAB&biw=1264&bih=431&dpr=2

Bonus Chapter—Chapter 11

34   Gravesen, G. (2017). *10 Seconds of Insane Courage*. Friendsville, TX: Baxter Press.

35   Theresa, M. (1968). *Anyway*. November 28, 2022. www.
      prayerfoundation.org.

Acknowledgments

36   Crosby, F. (1875). To God Be the Glory. In *Songs of
      Devotion* (Hymnal). Chicago, IL: Biglow & Main.

About the Author

Photo Credit: Caleb Jones Photography

HOLLY CURBY WAS born in Missouri and moved to Utah when she was four years old for her father's pastoral ministry. She is a single mother of two children, Allee and Peyton.

Holly became a Christian when she was seven years old. She has served in many areas of ministry: youth director and drama director (writing plays and directing community dinner theaters), directed the fellowship activities, discipleship training, Moms of Munchkins, and Women's Retreats. Holly has served as a deaconess and on the church outreach team. She has taught children, youth, and adult classes, and has been a group lead counselor in the AWANA ministry and member of the worship praise team at church.

Holly has her master's degree in management and leadership from Western Governor's University, is a graduate of the University of Utah with a bachelor of science degree in mass communication, and has an associate of science degree in public relations. Holly is also a graduate of the Fellows Leadership program affiliated with the Chick-fil-A Inc Foundation, is a certified life coach, and has many certificates of completion including travel and tourism, marketing from international shopping centers, youth director and drama director from Lifeway Christian Resources, a business class from HarvardX (initiative of Harvard University), and has been a certified cruise specialist with many cruise lines.

Holly has been in the marketing field for over twenty-five years, having served as assistant marketing manager and marketing director of local shopping malls, then as the events and sponsorships director for city chambers. She even served as an olympic liaison officer with the International Sports Broadcasting during the 2002 Olympics in Salt Lake City, Utah. Presently, Holly is the director of culture and community for two Chick-fil-A franchises in Utah.

Holly has received many accolades for her leadership and community involvement, including Inspirational Award from the Chick-fil-A Foundation, Volunteer of the Year from her former church in West Valley City, Utah, Business Champion of the Year from ChamberWest Chamber of Commerce, and Employee of the Year from Macerich Company's Intermountain Region.

Holly presently does public speaking at Women's Ministry events, including retreats, conferences, and special events. She has also emceed women's business conferences and spoken at city official meetings and many school events. Holly is also the host of *Holly's Highlights*, a podcast designed to encourage, inspire, and equip listeners to intentionally live their life full of purpose. Holly is a contributing writer to *Lifeway Journey* women's devotional and writes a monthly *Holly's Highlights* column in the local Utah paper, the *City Journals.*

Holly enjoys being with her family, traveling, watching movies, game nights, dining anywhere with patio seating, and simply getting to know people in an intimate setting—especially if it involves a porch swing.

Let's Connect!

- 🌀 **Website:** www.HollyCurby.com

- 🌀 **Email:** hello@HollyCurby.com

- 🌀 **Facebook:** www.Facebook.com/HollysHighlights

- 🌀 **Instagram:** @hollycurby

- 🌀 **Twitter:** @HollyCurby

- 🌀 **LinkedIn:** @HollyCurby

- 🌀 **TikTok:** @hollyshighlights

To inquire about having Holly speak at your event, or to schedule one-on-one coaching, visit: www.hollycurby.com/work-with-me.

Hopefully you found this book encouraging during your season of life. Your referral or purchase of *Face-Lift* for a friend and/or family member is one of the highest compliments I could receive.

TO HEAR MORE from Holly, check out *Holly's Highlights* podcast—a podcast designed to encourage, inspire, and equip you to intentionally live your life full of purpose.

Interested in sponsoring an episode, being a guest on the show, or inviting Holly to be a guest on your show? Simply visit **www.hollycurby.com/hollyshighlightspodcast** for more info.

A portion of all *Face-Lift* proceeds will be donated to Huntsman Cancer Institute. Thank you for helping make a difference in the fight against cancer.

The magic of Huntsman Cancer Institute (HCI) is that it instills hope. Hope for an effective treatment. Hope for a durable remission. Hope for one more holiday spent with loved ones. HCI's mission is to eradicate cancer from the face of the earth. How are we going to do it? Together.

By funding efforts to better understand the beginnings of cancer and more effectively treat cancer, Huntsman Cancer Foundation (HCF) helps relieve suffering and improve the quality of life for cancer patients, survivors, and their families. HCF encourages cancer patients, caregivers, and donors to come together in a myriad of ways to fight cancer individually and collectively through fundraising.

Huntsman Cancer Foundation
500 Huntsman Way
Salt Lake City, UT 84108-1235
huntsmancancer.org
1-801-584-5800
Huntsman Cancer Foundation (HCF) is a 501(c)(3)
organization
EIN: 87-0541293
Contributions are tax deductible to the extent permitted by
law.

Notes